DEBT VIRUS

DEBT VIRUS

*A Compelling Solution
to the
World's Debt Problems*

Jacques S. Jaikaran, M.D.

Glenbridge Publishing Ltd.

This book is designed to provide the author's findings and opinions based upon research and analysis of the subject matter covered. This information is not provided for purposes of rendering legal services, which can only be provided by knowledgeable attorneys.

Therefore, the author and publisher disclaim any responsibility for any liability or loss incurred as a consequence of the use and application, either directly or indirectly, of any advice or information presented herein.

Second Printing

Library of Congress Catalog Card Number: 91-70030

International Standard Book Number: 0-944435-13-0

To

My wife, Suhaila, for her devotion to me and our children during the many hours I was away from them researching world monetary systems. Her encouragement and support kept me going, in spite of the anger I experienced in discovering the truth about how the world's population has been enslaved by the money creators. I award her a medal of honor.

My son, F. René, and my daughter, Nicole, who first sparked the idea for this book when they asked me to explain money on Christmas day eight years ago. Little did I know then that this project would demand so much of my time. I commend them for their patience and understanding.

And to all the children of the world, that they will live to witness an intelligent and equitable monetary system, the abolishment of most taxes, and a planet free from hunger, disease, poverty, and wars. May they have the courage to complete the path to world peace and plenty that I envision for them.

CONTENTS

Foreword

Debt Virus is an intriguing book that questions the traditional role of money in our economy. It critically examines
the current money-creation process as the source of instability in the United States and global economies. Debt-ridden
money, laced with interest rate premiums, according to the
author, is a deadly virus which destroys the economic foundations of society in that total debt repayment is mathematically impossible. The debt virus is no respecter of governments, institutions, or individuals as it takes its toll on savings, investment, employment, income, growth, and stability. Inflation, recession, and economic depression are inevitable in an all-debt monetary system, and conventional explanations of these economic phenomena are grossly inadequate.

Debt money is the machination of financiers who, as
heirs to the goldsmiths of the Middle Ages, tend to conceal
the true meaning of money from the public. Most of our
money is created out of thin air with the stroke of a pen or
computer key rather than by the Treasury's printing press
that is actually controlled by the privately owned Federal
Reserve banks. The United States currency, coins, and checks
fall into this rubric as they are not full-bodied money, though
the government decrees it to be so, and economic agents

ix

readily accept it. *Debt Virus* questions the traditional method of money creation and unequivocally demonstrates its flaws.

A flawed monetary system can devastate a nation's economic health. Given the functions of money as a medium of exchange and as a unit of account, its effective management is vital to a nation's stability, growth, and equity. The government of Guernsey, a British protectorate in the Channel Islands, creates and spends interest-free money for public expenditures. Unlike Guernsey, the privately owned Federal Reserve System and its interlocking network of financiers and depository institutions, over which the United States government has absolutely no real control, consciously influence the money supply and hence the real gross national product. A byproduct of this enterprise is ever-mounting debt.

Public debt has only a remote possibility of repayment and imposes enormous potential burdens on present and future generations. *Debt Virus* mathematically advances this argument and concludes that unpayable debt, both public and private, leads to death and destruction as in the ancient civilizations of Egypt, Persia, Babylon, Greece, and the Roman Empire. The same fate awaits the United States economy, and indeed the world economy, if corrective measures are not taken to eradicate the infectious nature of debt money. Such a catastrophe, the author contends, is likely to occur by the year 2012.

The National Treasury should have the sole responsibility of creating money and clearing checks, all toward the mutual benefit of all economic agents, namely, households, businesses, and governments. Under a reformed system advocated by Jaikaran, government will create debt-free money for public expenditures and debt money for private expenditures. The money supply then would grow at a rate consistent with the needs of these agents so as to avoid undue economic fluctuations, defaults, bankruptcies, and foreclosures. A debt-free monetary system would eventually lead to "economic liberty" and an uninterrupted prosperity because there would be no shortage of money.

Debt Virus challenges the orthodox methods of money creation and its management in the United States economy and offers a compelling and convincing alternative to the status quo. *Debt Virus* undoubtedly is provocative and imperative reading for all who are concerned about the future of mankind.

Ashton I. Veramallay, Director,
Center for Economic Education,
Indiana University East

ACKNOWLEDGMENTS

I wish to acknowledge three special individuals who helped make this book possible. The group dynamics that were created among the four of us will continue through a company, Global Monetary Consultants, whose objective is to consult with governments about their monetary systems so that future generations need not suffer the inequities of the currently flawed systems.

To Glen B. Bowen for facilitating this project. Through his insight and vision, four individuals became a synergistic team with a common and higher goal. His selfless contribution of time, talent, and resources led to the transformation of an idea into tangible fruition. His gift of positive thought and his belief in this project were unwavering lessons in faith and friendship.

To Ben Johnston for his steadfast commitment to this project and for bringing his total dedication to the group that brought this book to completion. His expertise in financial investments, his experience as a writer and communicator, and his ability to think clearly about—and to challenge—the unique ideas put forth in this book all contributed to the transformation of my seven years of research and writings into a comprehensive treatise on global monetary systems.

To Nancy R. Olson for the many contributions she made to this project and to our group. She helped rewrite and edit the manuscript, she searched for and found our publisher, she helped negotiate the publishing contract, and she spent countless hours preparing the manuscript in its final form. In addition to contributing her time and numerous talents, it was a special privilege for us to share Nancy's bright mind, spontaneous humor, boundless energy, and wonderful spirit throughout this project.

In addition, I wish to thank the following who contributed their time and expertise in assembling information for this book: M. J. Brown, States Treasurer, Bailiwick of Guernsey; Professor Stephen K. Huber, Law School, University of Houston; and Professor Ashton Veramallay, Director of Economic Education, University of Indiana and Indiana State Economist.

Introduction

The money creators, through ignorance or design, have withheld the true facts about money from the public and their actions serve to dispossess humankind of wealth, property and freedom.

Envision a world without poverty or economic oppression, a place where humankind can attain its potential amidst the weightlessness of true freedom. Imagine the United States, and the rest of the world, without hunger or homelessness, where educated societies enjoy all the fruits of their labor. In such a society it wouldn't be necessary to hand over your hard-earned dollars to the government to pay ever-increasing taxes. Could you learn to live in a place where budgets were balanced, homes were affordable, and you kept all the money you earned?

Utopian? Maybe. Unattainable? Perfection always is. But our planet desperately needs to make some changes before it's too late.

In the United States, the richest country on earth both in tangible assets and natural resources, people can't afford health care. Currently, there are reportedly forty million

1

Americans without health insurance. Many are living from paycheck to paycheck—if they have a paycheck at all. Our public or government debt is rising so rapidly that the annual interest on it will exceed the money in circulation before long. How did we allow all this to occur?

Elementary economics textbooks concede that when banks make loans or investments, they create money. This money is given many fancy names like "bank credit," "checkbook money," and "demand deposit" by bankers. The academicians call it the "monetization" of debt, meaning that debt is converted into money. Specifically, the monetization of debt is the creation of checkbook money through bank loans or investments.

The monetization of debt can be illustrated by examining the roots of modern banking. Ancient goldsmiths made jewelry for kings, lords, princes, and wealthy merchants. To manufacture these items, goldsmiths kept small reserves of gold in their vaults. Because goldsmiths had facilities for storing the precious metal, other people began to bring their gold to the artisans for safekeeping. In return, the goldsmiths would charge a small fee to cover storage costs. When the deposits were made, the people requested receipts; the goldsmiths would only return the gold when the receipts for the gold were presented to them.

If the gold was in the form of uniform bars, people did not care what gold was returned to them as long as they got back comparable gold bars when they presented their receipts. By not having to keep track of who owned which bars, goldsmiths minimized their storage costs.

Goldsmiths soon discovered that only a small amount of gold was needed to accommodate the gold withdrawals on any given day. People seldom requested their gold, which was collecting dust in the back room under lock and key.

Instead, they used the gold receipts to transact their business in the marketplace. This practice became more and more widespread because people found it more convenient to use storage receipts for transactions instead of heavy gold.

Although the storage receipts were mere pieces of paper, they were accepted as a medium of exchange; they were received in the same way as circulating gold. As long as goldsmiths kept the gold in back rooms, the money supply in the marketplace included whatever gold was in circulation (outside the goldsmiths' vaults) plus the receipts for gold.

One day a friend of a goldsmith suggested a method—presumably illegal—of making additional profits. The friend proposed that, since all the gold in the back room was gathering dust, he lend some of it out at interest.

In exchange for an IOU, the goldsmith gave the friend some gold. The moment this transaction occurred, the money supply was increased by the amount of the loan. At that point, the money supply consisted of storage receipts, the gold previously in circulation, and the gold loaned out by the goldsmith. The goldsmith monetized debt by giving out gold in exchange for the borrower's IOU. The goldsmith's friend, of course, could have taken a receipt for the gold rather than the gold itself since storage receipts served the same purpose in the marketplace.

Thus was born our modern-day banking system. Doesn't it seem odd that, despite our many modern inventions and newfound capabilities, our banking system is still patterned after the ancient goldsmith system that present-day economists concede monetizes debt?

Michael Milken made billions converting equity into debt by providing highly leveraged financing through his high-yield bonds—a medium he "invented" in the early

1980s. Milken subsequently entered a guilty plea to certain transgressions relating to his activities.

Let us examine the Milken "invention." He took small amounts of equity in companies and magnified or expanded that equity by converting it into debt, debt that carried a higher than normal interest charge because it was highly leveraged. You can call his invention the "fractional debt expansion system."

Now let's look at the banking system in similar terms. Commercial banks take small amounts of equity (the true deposits of their customers) and routinely convert this equity into debt—highly leveraged debt—based on the constraints of their fractional reserve requirements. This debt is called "money" by the bankers, but in reality it is money they owe.

Is there any significant difference between what banks routinely do and what Mr. Milken "invented"? Both techniques involve debt and leveraging. In Milken's case, his Wall Street firm ceased to exist, and Milken was forced out of the securities industry in disgrace; but our banks encounter no similar fate.

In the case of savings and loans, which were allowed to function as banks concurrently with Milken's invention of the "junk bond," the full scope of the debacle is yet to be realized. It is safe to say that the savings and loan bail out will cost American taxpayers hundreds of billions of dollars. This event could have been avoided had the awesome impact of highly leveraged debt been fully understood. In truth, our entire monetary system is based on debt. The United States government issues bonds at an interest charge and therefore burdens the taxpayers when it just as easily could issue interest-free currency to accomplish the same task.

Practically every single American dollar in existence is

born as debt, yet we go blissfully on our way ignorant of the crisis that we ultimately must confront.

I was born and grew up in Guyana, a third-world country on the northern coast of South America. As a barefoot youth, I wielded a machete as a laborer cutting sugar cane on a plantation. As a young adult, I spent ten years in England, attending college and medical school. Another seven years were spent in America honing my skills to become first a fully trained general surgeon, then a board-certified plastic surgeon. Now I have an active practice of cosmetic and reconstructive plastic surgery in Humble, Texas, within the municipal boundaries of Houston.

Several years ago, I was invited to join the board of directors of a local bank. While assuming this task, I became perplexed by the inconsistencies confronting me. Consequently, I embarked on a study of global monetary systems. For seven years I studied the monetary systems of the world. In the process, I uncovered a flaw in our monetary system that poses a serious threat to society—a flaw first recognized long ago by the Greek philosopher, Aristotle.

In the process of preparing this manuscript, I frequently encountered skeptical attitudes. After all, "how could a physician claim to be an expert on money?" I studied seventeen years after high school to become a qualified plastic surgeon, and I have spent seven years studying global monetary systems. When I walk into an operating room, a certification process grants me privileges and obligations to operate as a board-certified surgeon. Unfortunately, there is no such parallel course available to me as a monetary scientist. No certification exists for the knowledge I have acquired about global monetary systems. Therefore, I come to you as a cane cutter, a plastic surgeon, and a fellow citizen, submitting that truth, logic, and reasoning are sufficient without portfolio. And I challenge everyone—experts and all—to refute the scientific conclusions I have reached in this work.

My proposals are workable. In fact, a hybrid system has been tested for about 170 years on the bailiwick of Guernsey and for a little less time on Jersey, another bailiwick in the Channel Islands. I visited Guernsey and have personally collected some of the data contained in this book.

In the course of my research, I have had the privilege of corresponding with Dr. Milton Friedman, the major proponent of monetarism. The highly respected Dr. Friedman argues that, "inflation is always and everywhere a monetary phenomenon, and inflation cannot persist unless it is supported by monetary growth." According to Friedman, supply-side inflation is just a temporary phenomenon, important only in the short run. The major cause of inflation is demand-pull, and demand-pull is caused by excessive monetary growth.

Dr. Friedman appears to ignore the all-debt characteristic of our money creation process. He has not dealt with this problem in a scientific manner in any of his writings. When asked about the concept of debt-free money he replied, "Federal Reserve Notes in the Treasury and gold from the California gold fields were debt-free money." But gold was never truly used as money, and a "note" by its very nature is a debt.

The root cause of a major part of our monetary problems is that money is created as debt and is subject to an interest charge. This interest charge is the cause of inflation, which leads to the debasement or decrease in purchasing power (devaluation) of our currency.

The process of money creation is discussed in great detail in the body of this book, but for now, assume I am correct in saying that the creation process used by the banks in this country is exactly parallel to the process I outlined in the beginning of this introduction—the monetization of debt.

When money is created as debt, is the interest charge owed on that money likewise created? The answer is no, and this is the crux of the problem in our all-debt monetary system. This flaw dooms our present system to failure, not only in the United States but also for the rest of the globe. It is speeding our day of judgment unless entirely new corrective measures are taken.

To illustrate, let us assume that we use milk as currency. Someone—without our knowledge—dilutes our milk (money) supply with water, and we end up with considerably more diluted milk in the money supply than when we started. The likely result is that someone will discover that the milk has been watered down and will demand a larger quantity of the diluted milk in exchange for goods or services.

In an all-debt money system, how does money become "watered down" or lose its purchasing power? Let's assume that over the last eight years the merchant has changed his asking price for a loaf of bread from $1.00 to $1.50. Assume also that there has been no change in the size of the loaf; it is identical to the first loaf. What has occurred? A 50 percent decline in the purchasing power of money has been brought about because of the increased asking price of the loaf of bread.

This is what the Consumer Price Index (CPI) measures—the increase in the asking price of products. Note that it does not measure the cost of those products but only the increase in the asking price of those products. By asking for more debt money for the same product, the purchasing power of money decreases. Through this process our money loses its purchasing power in the marketplace and is "watered down."

When there is an increase in the prices of goods and services in the economic arena, a relative shortage of purchasing power occurs. More money will then be needed in the economy to continue exchanging the same goods and services. Otherwise, many goods and services will go unsold, the consequences of which will also be dealt with in great detail later in this book.

In an all-debt money system, additional borrowing at interest to increase the money supply is necessary to restore full purchasing power in the marketplace. Although in truth there is an increase in the money supply, is it fair to say that this *increase* in the money supply caused the inflation? No. More accurately, it was the *decrease* in purchasing power— the *devaluation* caused by asking more money for the same product and services that caused it.

In an all-debt money system, it is the nonproductive interest payments—a cost of doing business—that leads to asking more money for the same products and services. This mechanism is thus the root source of inflation, and it will be fully illustrated in a later chapter.

Our central banking system, contrary to mainstream thinking, is privately owned. When our government needs money beyond what it collects in taxes, it prints bonds, which are interest-bearing instruments, and uses them as collateral to borrow money from the private banking industry, which literally creates money out of thin air. As preposterous as it sounds, this is exactly how money is created by the privately owned banking system.

In 1975 the United States government debt was $475 billion, and today it is over $3 trillion. This debt has been increasing exponentially. With a current debt of over $3 trillion, it is not hard to extrapolate what the magnitude of government debt in the United States will be over the next twenty years. Worse yet, this problem is only one of many in an all-debt money system.

The ever-changing purchasing power of our currency, in effect, gives us an "elastic foot" for measuring our work effort. After all, we do not work for money. We work so that our output can be exchanged for the output of other productive members of society. We use money as a convenient medium of exchange and as a unit of measurement for this output. We should expect some stability in this unit of exchange, but the element of inflation is constantly changing its purchasing power.

Can you imagine a carpenter working with an "elastic foot" measure? One week the ceiling is eight feet high; the next week the foot measure has contracted and in "real" terms the ceiling is measured at eight feet and six inches. This is pure nonsense of course, but we endure similar nonsense in our "elastic" monetary system when the unit of measurement—the dollar—is continually shrinking.

In 1822, on the island of Guernsey, the citizens decided to construct a market, and that market still stands today. What makes this market unique is how it was financed. The economic climate of Guernsey today is a direct result of that financing plan. The following inscription was taken directly from a plaque at the site of the structure:

> In 1820 the States agreed to build a covered market for £5,500. As they had one thousand pounds in hand, 4,500 notes of one pound each were issued on the security of a small tax on spirituous liquors. The work was undertaken and the market complete and opened in 1822.
>
> Each of the 36 shops yielded £5 in rent. As soon as the £180 was received each year, 180 states' notes were burnt. The 4,500 notes would have taken too long to

destroy at this rate but the States also paid into the market fund £300 per annum derived from tax on wines coming into the island.

£30 of this were set aside for running repairs and £270 went toward the extinction of more paper notes.

At the end of ten years, not one of the notes issued to pay for the building was left, no interest had been paid upon them and there was a steady income of £180.

Guernsey currently circulates £13 million of Guernsey coin and paper currency, fully redeemable by the state's Treasury. They are redeemable in Bank of England notes, which are not backed by gold or silver, but rather by collateral put up to create such notes into existence. Guernsey money is debt money, but it is not issued at interest. Guernsey currency is similar in character to the $431 million "Lincoln Greenbacks" issued during the Civil War.

Guernsey has a 20 percent income tax, zero unemployment, and a very high standard of living. The money supply has increased 40 percent in real terms during the past three years. The Guernsey government spends these notes directly into the Guernsey economy for public expenditures and without interest charge to the Treasury.

Although inflation in Guernsey has been running at about 9 percent, this rate is much lower than in the British Isles of which Guernsey is a protectorate. The fact that the money supply has increased 40 percent in real terms indicates that the quality of service in Guernsey is improving at a rate greater than the inflation rate, since money is being put into circulation, interest free, for government expenditures instead of being borrowed at interest.

Because Guernsey is an island and the island depends on imports, there are certain external factors that have a strong influence on its inflation rate. Gasoline costs £2 per gallon in England and £1 per gallon in Guernsey. A ten pence tax on £2 thus factors out as a 5 percent increase in the cost of British gasoline but a 10 percent increase on Guernsey gasoline.

During 1990, the average family income on Guernsey was £40,000: there were approximately sixty-four thousand residents and in excess of forty-three thousand cars on the island. The average home now costs about £140,000. Living costs are far lower than living costs in the British Isles, and as you would suspect, there are some restrictions about taking up a new residence in Guernsey. When asked how the Guernsey Treasury can create and spend money interest free for public expenditures, M. J. Brown, states treasurer of the Bailiwick of Guernsey, commented to me, "There is nothing written down that allows us to do what we do, but no one questions us about it."

Through study and research, I have reached the conclusion that the money creation process should be controlled by the government and not be under the domain of private elements, as is the case in the United States. I am not alone in this view. In a "Primer on Money" published in 1954, Dr. Milton Friedman proposed that the Treasury issue all money and that we adopt a system of 100 percent reserves. The fractional reserve deposit expansion money system we employ, in concert with debt-money issued at interest, is the root of several monumental economic problems facing our society.

Let's embark on an examination of our monetary system. We will logically examine a system borne from an arcane goldsmith system, and we will pinpoint where we can make changes to contain the virus of an all-debt money system that wreaks havoc throughout the world. Debt in itself is not bad; it is debt with interest that is the uncontrollable and deadly virus that leads to inflation, economic recession, economic depression, bankruptcies, business failures, and all the consequent social ills of unemployment.

The lack of money is the source of many of our economic and social problems today. Yet, we have the power to change the devastation that the lack of money causes before it is too late. We can exercise our inalienable right to improve what critically needs improvement. The future of our country depends on it. Our children deserve a better system than the one we inherited. The undesirable alternative is a "New World Order" controlled by the international financiers.

That's what this book is about—the devastating consequences of the design flaw in our monetary system. Our monetary system appears complex, but it can be approached scientifically. It can be taken apart, reduced to its component parts, and analyzed so that we can better understand its character.

Our money is born out of debt, and its all-debt character is causing staggering amounts of debt to pile up; however, it is impossible totally to wipe out all debts under our present system. To understand the folly of attempting to wipe out total debt, one must first understand the fundamentals of money.

This book will help you to understand where we are, how we got there, the dangerous direction toward which we are heading, and what steps we can take to avert a catastrophe before it occurs sometime in the year 2012, or possibly earlier. By that time, the current dollar will be worthless because of the continuing erosion of purchasing power.

Let us lift the shroud of secrecy that envelops the aristocracy of banking. The money creators, those powerful few who control the very lifeblood of society, are the financiers whose policies have shaped the fates of kings, nations, and of all civilization. The system within which they operate is based upon a fundamental error that originated with the very conception of the banking system. This flaw has caused astronomical sums of money to flow directly into bank coffers, where it is jealously guarded by undeserving present-day heirs to the system.

As with all innovative ideas, the concepts outlined in this book may at first seem complex. But the reader who maintains an open mind and a sincere desire to understand the machinations of this intricate system will be rewarded with new insights and abundant information about how to change the system for the benefit of all humankind.

Chapter 1

What's Wrong With Debt?

*I am not afraid to be eccentric in my opinion. Was not
every opinion now accepted once eccentric?*

The Philadelphia winter of 1765 was cold. Heat from an
odd-looking appliance filled the room as the man in the
chair wrinkled his brow and peered through his eyeglasses
at the sheet on his lap desk.

"If I keep a penny instead of spending it," he mused,
"there is a one hundred percent alteration in my holdings. I
go from nothing to the sum of one."

Two years earlier, this thoughtful gentleman had visited
England. When asked why trade in the American colonies
was prospering, Ben Franklin had replied, "Our prosperity is
simple, we issue our own money. It is called 'Colonial
Scrip' and it facilitates the exchange of goods." He went on
to explain that when it became apparent that trade in the
colonies was being hampered because of the lack of an
appropriate medium of exchange, a medium was devised

and issued by the governors of the various colonies. Since there was an abundance of produce and goods available, great prosperity came to the colonies with this new release of adequate purchasing power. Once an easy exchange was possible, the colonies thrived.

Soon this information was brought to the attention of the Rothschilds. This canny European banking family recognized the opportunity to exploit an emerging nation. The Rothschilds' bank arranged for a bill to be introduced into the English Parliament that denied any English colony the right to issue its own money—English money had to be used. The colonies were consequently compelled to discard their "Scrip" and mortgage themselves to the Bank of England. For the first time, our money began to be based on debt. In 1780, only sixteen years after the enactment of this law by the English Parliament, there was a great economic recession in America.

So began the flaw in our monetary system, the effects of which are all too familiar to us today.

What About Inflation?

In December 1987, I attended a seminar at a local college. The subject was the stock market crash of October 1987. The participating panelists at this seminar were men who managed large sums of money at three major investment firms in Houston. During the course of the discussion, I asked, "What causes inflation in our economy?"

"Inflation is caused by the government printing large sums of money to finance its expenditures," one replied.

I asked if he really believed this statement to be true. Though somewhat annoyed, he politely answered, "Yes."

He added that he had been taught this throughout college—including postgraduate courses in economics.

So that there could be no misconceptions in the audience, I restated my question, "You are saying, sir, that the government creates money for its expenditures. Is that true?"

"Yes," he replied, "that's exactly what I mean."

There was silence in the audience as several of those attending gazed in my direction, awaiting my response. *"If you had either the privilege, the right, or the power to create money that you needed for your expenditures, would you ever be in debt, sir?"* I asked.

His expression changed—a quizzical look appeared on his face. He flushed slightly and mumbled, "I guess not."

Tension invaded the room as more quizzical looks flashed randomly onto faces in the audience. I continued, "Well, sir, if the government is creating the money to finance its expenditures, could you please explain to me why the government is in debt to the tune of more than two and one-half trillion dollars?"

He looked toward his companions on the panel. It was apparent that my questions disturbed them since they had corroborated the first economist's statements. They had all previously claimed that inflation is caused by too much money being created by the government, which in turn spends the money to cover its own expenses. It seemed obvious that the answer given by the economists to explain the cause of inflation was wrong! These two statements, "The government creates money to finance its expenditures," and, "The government has a debt of more than $2.5 trillion," cannot both be true. We know that the debt is a fact; therefore, the former statement must be false.

Money does not occur naturally in the universe—it cannot be mined, cultivated, or fished from the ocean. Its existence requires the active involvement of man. But if money is not an element of nature and the government does not create it, then who does create money in the United States? Is all you have been taught about inflation true?

Recession

In the *Great Depression of 1990*, Dr. Ravi Batra observes, "As soon as aggregate demand falls for any reason, some goods go unsold because inventories rise, output falls, and some workers are laid off. A few businesses and banks begin to fail. This, of course, typically occurs during a recession."[1] Dr. Batra rightly states that a contraction in demand for goods and services is what eventually leads to a recession. However, the fundamental question has not been asked by Dr. Batra and other contemporary economists: "What is the *cause of the contraction in the demand* for goods and services?"

The *Story of Money*, by D. H. Friedman and C. J. Parnow, clearly states that recessions are the result of a shortage of money in the economy.[2] But, if money is not an element of nature, it must be created by man. No special materials are required to make it, and, since 1968, money has not been backed by anything. Why, then, is there a shortage of money during a recession? The mechanics of this shortage will be fully explained later.

Depression

An economic depression is a severe economic recession. If an economic recession is caused by a shortage of money in the economy, then a depression must be caused by a severe shortage of money in the economy. Dr. Batra claims in his work, "Economic depressions are caused by a concentration of wealth."[3] But such a notion is ludicrous.

If one examines this premise carefully, it becomes apparent that a concentration of wealth is no more a cause of depressions than a windmill is the cause of lusty gales. The concentration of wealth is only a symptom of an impending financial collapse. An absolute and severe shortage of money in the economy relative to the total prices of all existing goods and services is the cause of economic depressions.

During recessions and depressions, there are increased numbers of bankruptcies, foreclosures, and business failures as well as a rise in involuntary unemployment. But these are secondary events to the shortage of money. What is the mechanism that causes this shortage?

Rising Consumer Price Index

The consumer price index (CPI) measures how much a consumer spends on a typical market basket of goods and services at a certain point in time. By comparing one year's index with another, we can discover how much prices have moved up or down, thereby determining what has happened to the purchasing power of our unit of money—the dollar. Figure 1 shows that prices have been increasing almost steadily since 1900.

Assume that the price of a typical market basket of goods and services was $100 in 1967, the base year used by our current CPI. In 1900, this same market basket of goods and services cost $25. By 1930, the goods and services advanced in price to $50—twice that of the 1900 cost. By 1975, the same set of goods and services cost $161. In 1987, they cost $350.

EXPONENTIAL GROWTH OF CPI
SINCE 1900

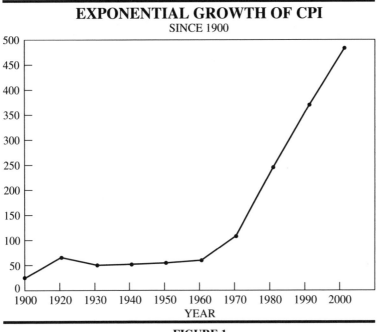

FIGURE 1

This graph makes it readily apparent that the CPI has been rising steadily for the last eighty years. This exponential curve, a curve that rises at an ever-increasing rate, reveals the inflation rate or the increase in the cost of goods and services. When the curve slopes upward gently, inflation is low—perhaps 1 or 2 percent. When the slope is steep, such as during the early 1980s, the inflation rate is greater than 10 percent.

It is evident that by September 1987 the price of the average market basket of goods and services had increased two and one-half times, or 250 percent since the base year of 1967. The rise in the CPI can also be a means to determine how quickly the purchasing power of the dollar is decreasing—in other words, at what rate the dollar is becoming worthless. When will the 1900 dollar become totally void of purchasing power?

TABLE 1
RISE OF CPI SINCE 1900

Year	CPI = 100 in 1967
1900	25
1920	60
1930	50
1950	55
1967	100
1975	161
1981	272
1983	287
1987 (Sept)	345

Declining Purchasing Power

From Table 1, we can readily see that the same goods and services that cost one dollar in 1967 could be purchased for twenty-five cents in 1900, or 25 percent of the base-year cost. It is logical to conclude that the dollar in 1900 bought four times as much as the same dollar in 1967.

$$100/CPI = 100/25 = 4$$

By dividing 100 by the CPI, for each of the years in Table 1, a tabular representation of the collapse of the purchasing power of the dollar since 1900 can be obtained (Table 2).

TABLE 2
PURCHASING POWER OF DOLLAR BASED
ON VALUE BEING ONE IN 1967

Year	Purchasing Power
1900	$4.00
1920	1.67
1930	2.00
1950	1.82
1967	1.00
1975	0.62
1981	0.37
1983	0.33
1987 (Sept)	0.29

TABLE 3
PURCHASING POWER OF DOLLAR BASED
ON VALUE BEING $1.00 IN 1900

Year	Purchasing Power
1900	$1.00
1920	0.42
1930	0.50
1950	0.45
1967	0.25
1975	0.16
1981	0.09
1983	0.08
1987 (Sept)	0.07

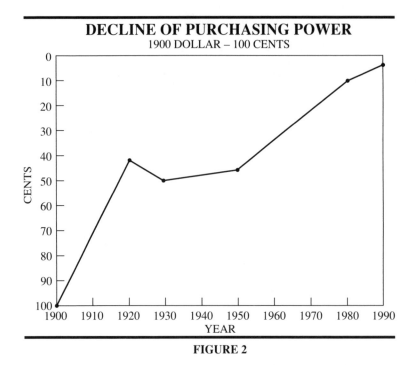

DECLINE OF PURCHASING POWER
1900 DOLLAR – 100 CENTS

FIGURE 2

The 1987 dollar was worth about twenty-nine cents in comparison to the 1967 dollar, but it lost an astonishing 92.75 percent in purchasing power since 1900. In other words, the 1900 dollar would purchase more than thirteen times as much goods and services as the 1987 dollar.

The data in Table 3 was derived by dividing the purchasing power in Table 2 by 4 to show the current purchasing power of the 1900 dollar. This provides a tabular picture of what has happened to the purchasing power of money since 1900. If the rate of decline in purchasing power for the 1900 dollar had continued at a rate similar to that between the years 1950 and 1983, the 1900 dollar would have been worthless by 1990. But since 1983, the decrease in the purchasing power of the dollar has slowed down somewhat (Figure 2).

Inflation in the early part of the twentieth century, beginning about 1914 and continuing until 1920, was due in large part to World War I. The CPI doubled during these years from 30 to 60, which meant that the purchasing power of the dollar declined by 100 percent. (Purchasing power is the reciprocal, the mathematical opposite, of the CPI.) Where has this purchasing power gone?

Social Ills

Poverty, hunger, and disease have plagued this planet since the dawn of history. We are bombarded daily with appeals for these causes. It is inconceivable that on a planet so rich in natural resources there are still millions of people dying of starvation.

It has been said that the love of money is the root of all evil. An attentive observer would conclude that it is the *lack* of money that is more likely the root of evil. Most crimes are committed not by people who are fully employed, well clothed, well fed, and adequately housed, but by those in economic need.

In the overwhelming majority of divorce cases in the United States, the lack of money is cited as the main reason for discord. The divorce rate is at an all-time high, with at least one in three marriages ending in divorce or separation within the first five years of marriage.

Throughout history, civilizations have been plagued by inflation, recession, and depression. Since these periods have occurred in a cyclical fashion, there is a tendency to blame economic problems on natural forces. But the cycles of nature are uniform and occur with undeviating uniformity. The cycles of inflation, recession, and depression do not possess such a uniformity. Inflation, depression, and a precipitous decline in the purchasing power of the dollar are only symptoms of a deeper problem.

Consider these historical events:

> When ancient Egypt fell, only 4 percent of the population held all the wealth.

> When the Babylonian civilization collapsed, only 3 percent of the people owned all the wealth.

> When ancient Persia was destroyed, 2 percent of the people owned all the wealth.

> When ancient Greece sank into ruin, only 0.5 percent of the people held all the wealth.

> When the Roman Empire collapsed into ruin, only about two thousand people owned all the wealth in the known civilized world, and this debacle ushered in the period of history known as the Dark Ages.

Yet we continue to repeat the basic mistake that contributed to the collapse of these civilizations with an alarming air of ignorance.

The most recent economic catastrophe occurred in France in the 1790s. Between 1790 and 1795, the price of a bushel of flour rose from $ 0.40 to $45. A cart of wood that previously cost $4. demanded $500., and a pair of shoes climbed in price from $1. to $40. During this period, the public debt at interest also increased tremendously.

Grave ills beset the French monetary system during this period. Napoleon rose to power when the middle class went bankrupt. It took more than forty years for France to recover from its financial collapse, a collapse that triggered the French Revolution.

All-Debt Monetary System

The element woven into our economic fabric that leads to inflation, recession, depression, business failure, a rising consumer price index, and the decreased purchasing power of the dollar is nothing more mysterious than our *all-debt monetary system.*

Economists never actually talk about the debt-money system or the fundamental mechanics of money. They have done an admirable job in their own right, but their conclusions have not been based on a full and complete appreciation of the facts. Though money management is taught, precise money mechanics is not examined at any level of our educational system. What is even more astonishing is that no one even bothers to ask why this is so. This book examines the fundamental flaw in our monetary system and supplies information that will allow accurate conclusions to be drawn by each and every one of us.

In the words of Oliver Goldsmith, "Ill fares the land, to hastening ills a prey. Where wealth accumulates and men decay." The most pernicious of all viruses is the one that confiscates the wealth of the productive elements of society and transfers it to the hands of a nonproductive few.

Chapter 2

Ultimate Secrets

They say that knowledge is power. I used to think so, but now I know that they mean Money.

Lord Byron

The terms "wealth" and "money" are often used interchangeably, but in reality they are not the same thing. Wealth is derived from things with physical substance and intrinsic value. It is created from the elements nature provides, through the use of our hands or the help of machinery. A home, food, and clothing are examples of wealth. We need these things for our survival, or at least to make our lives more comfortable.

Money has no intrinsic value. Like the tape measure in the hands of the carpenter, it is a means of measurement. As such, it has no value other than to gauge the wealth an individual controls. A person isolated on a desert island with all the money he wants, will soon find out that it cannot be mortared in place to build a home, nor can it be worn or eaten.

Money

Money is any generally accepted medium of exchange, not simply coin and paper currency. It does not have to be intrinsically valuable or in any special form. In the past, items ranging from iron nails and dried codfish to gunpowder and tobacco have served as money. Its primary function is to activate production and facilitate the purchase and sale of goods and services. In addition, it provides a means to store wealth in a form other than real property.

In a sense, money is artificial. It is a creation of society—a "fiat" currency, backed by the government's ability to tax its citizens and the citizens' ability to produce goods and services. Only the goodwill and confidence of society make it acceptable as a medium of exchange. At one time, gold served as money. In the dim reaches of some forgotten past, this shiny metal was thought to have a special beauty and a high value. In reality, it served as money only because society decided that it would.

A Federal Reserve publication points out, "Money cannot feed, clothe, or shelter us. Only goods and services can satisfy these needs. The goal of economic activity is to provide ourselves with as many of life's necessities—and luxuries—as we can have."[1]

Functions of Money

Probably the most important functions of money as a medium of exchange are:

to activate the production of goods and services;

to facilitate the transfer of goods and services;

to pay taxes and debt; and,

to serve as a measure and store of value.

To facilitate its functions, money must be acceptable to all of us. We must accept it in payment for our work or in payment for the goods we produce and market, and we must be confident others will accept it when we need what they have.

Money does this job better when it is denominated in standard units like dollars and cents. It then gains usefulness as an expression of prices for goods and services. In this manner we can convert an hour's work into a measure of milk, a pair of shoes, shelter, or food.

From another perspective, we can use money as a form of claims on goods and services that we can "call" either now or in the future as we see fit.

Medium of Exchange in the United States

I was recently asked to speak before a group of high school seniors. "What, in your view, is money?" I asked the students. They responded with blank stares until someone ventured, "Money is a medium of exchange." I then asked, "What is the medium of exchange in the United States?" Several replied that money in the United States is coin and currency (Federal Reserve notes). I waited for additional answers, but none were forthcoming. I have asked the same question of economists, university educators, financial advisors, and bankers, and the answer is invariably the same: "Money is coins and Federal Reserve notes." This reply is not surprising since the fundamentals of money are not taught in schools or universities. It seems strange, however, that no more than a handful of people know the true nature of the medium of exchange they use on a daily basis and that impacts almost every aspect of their lives.

Coins and currency are not the only forms of money. Today we use coins, currency, and commercial bank demand deposits (checkbook money) as money. A publication by the Federal Reserve Bank of New York states: "Today Americans use several types of money: coins issued by the Treasury; paper currency issued by the Federal Reserve banks; checkable deposits of depository institutions such as demand deposits; automatic transfer accounts at commercial banks; share draft accounts at credit unions; and, negotiable orders of withdrawal (NOW accounts at savings banks and savings and loan associations). Money in these accounts can readily be used for transactions. The most common form is demand deposits."[2] Demand deposits, or checkbook money, comprise about 75 percent of all money in circulation.

From this information, it becomes clear that only coin is issued by the national Treasury. The rest of the money in circulation is created by Federal Reserve banks and all other banks.

Friedman and Parnow in their publication *The Story of Money* observe, "One institution, the commercial bank, creates the bulk of new money—checkbook money—when it lends or invests. Producers and workers borrowing from commercial banks put this new money into circulation. Thrifts also create money when they lend."[3] Thrifts are institutions such as savings banks, savings and loan associations, and credit unions.

In numerous discussions with friends and colleagues regarding money creation in the United States, time and time again I heard, "The government and that damn printing press; they are the ones printing all the money and causing inflation." Herein lies one of the fundamental misconceptions about our entire monetary system. Isn't it strange that, since the government (Treasury) has a printing press for printing Federal Reserve notes, nearly everyone assumes that the government spends what it prints for its expenditures. Why, then, is the government in debt for more than $3 trillion? The Federal Reserve Bank of New York explains:

"The Bureau of Engraving and Printing in Washington, D.C., a unit of the Treasury, is responsible for printing the nation's currency, but, its orders to print come from the twelve Federal Reserve banks, not the president or Congress. The Reserve banks, not the Treasury, determine how much currency is printed, based mainly on estimates of depository institutions and public cash demands. Under this arrangement, the government cannot print more Federal Reserve notes to pay its bills or reduce its debt."[4]

The Treasury only prints money when asked to do so by the Federal Reserve System, not unlike going to a print shop to have letterheads or business cards printed. The Treasury is the printer, not the spender. After it is printed, the fresh money is turned over to the Federal Reserve banks. But the Federal Reserve banks belong to the federal government, right? *Wrong!*

Federal Reserve banks are not governmental institutions. They are privately held corporations. All twelve Federal Reserve banks are privately owned banking institutions.

The Federal Reserve System

The Federal Reserve System was initially created to stabilize purchasing power and prevent economic recessions, depressions, bank failures, and financial panics. Often referred to simply as "The Fed," it is made up of a Board of Governors that is a governmental agency based in Washington, D.C. The Board of Governors consists of seven people appointed for fourteen-year terms by the president of the United States, with the advice and consent of the Senate. Although the board has the power to approve policies, it rarely, if ever, changes them, and it has quasi-supervisory control over the Federal Reserve System.

There are twelve regional banks, one for each of the twelve Federal Reserve districts into which the country is divided. These banks are private corporations chartered by Congress to operate the nation's central banking system. All nationally chartered banks and most large, state-chartered banks are members of the Federal Reserve System. They are known as "member banks."

One of the key committees in the system is the Federal Open Market Committee, which includes the seven members of the Board of Governors and five Federal Reserve bank presidents. This committee oversees the buying and selling of government securities in the open market, and thus increases or decreases the reserves of commercial banks.

The Federal Advisory Council is also part of the system. This group is composed of twelve people, each elected by the board of directors of a Federal Reserve bank. The nominees are usually from among bankers in their Reserve district. This council advises the Federal Reserve Board regarding the status of economic affairs in different regions of the country.

Ownership of the Federal Banks

The twelve regional Federal Reserve banks are not government institutions but are corporations nominally "owned" by member commercial banks, who must buy special, nonmarketable stock in their district Federal Reserve bank.[5]

EXHIBIT 1

3. EXEMPTION FROM TAXATION

"Federal reserve banks, including the capital stock and surplus therein, and the income derived therefrom shall be exempt from Federal, State, and local taxation, except taxes upon real estate."

(Federal Reserve Act, Board of Governors of the Federal Reserve, Section 7, Clause 3.)

Congress created the Federal Reserve in 1913, but Congress doesn't run its operations. Neither does the president of the United States. The Fed is an independent organization. When the Federal Reserve was created, its stock was sold to the member banks. The Fed earns interest on the government securities it owns. Out of this income it pays operating expenses and dividends to its stockholders, the member banks.

If you write a letter to any Federal Reserve bank or to any one of its branches, you will notice that the reply envelope is not franked. The bank will not have an official government stamp, whereas all government institutions usually use government-issued envelopes or stamps.

According to the Federal Reserve Act, Federal Reserve banks do pay real estate taxes.[6] Of course, we know that government-owned buildings are not assessed real estate taxes (see Exhibit 2).

One can also check the phone book in any city where a Federal Reserve bank is located (see Exhibit 3).

Under "Banks" in a telephone directory in any one of these cities—Boston, New York, Philadelphia, Cleveland,

EXHIBIT 2
INCOME AND EXPENSES OF FEDERAL
RESERVE BANKS, 1986
(Sample: 4 out of 12)

Dollars

Item	Total	Boston	New York	Philadelphia	Cleveland
Current Income					
Loans	279,190,611	1,120,763	4,896,983	2,018,391	674,180
U.S. Treasury and Federal agency securities	16,141,544,144	945,814,646	5,349,330,871	532,591,184	941,194,643
Foreign Currencies	393,563,826	11,816,759	97,225,032	18,089,170	23,594,141
Priced Services	627,736,431	40,112,790	91,705,355	27,488,236	38,173,956
Other	22,116,636	718,137	12,202,190	416,697	415,209
Total	**17,464,151,647**	**999,583,095**	**5,555,360,431**	**580,603,678**	**1,004,052,128**
Current Expenses					
Salaries and other personnel expenses	596,170,328	37,836,420	121,402,742	31,833,173	33,961,449
Retirements and other Benefits......	133,360,309	8,309,368	24,926,134	7,455,196	8,233,284
Fees	11,206,609	3,115,473	1,410,355	544,866	1,586,532
Travel	19,775,226	895,990	2,608,710	781,103	1,642,322
Postage and other shipping costs......	81,879,848	3,689,087	9,081,204	4,700,356	5,996,838
Communications	15,254,693	1,032,847	3,485,763	659,592	734,643
Materials and Supplies	46,004,715	2,647,573	8,607,238	2,702,203	2,958,404
Building Expenses					
Taxes on Real Estate	**22,213,256**	**4,049,382**	**3,942,496**	**1,484,083**	**1,032,263**
Property Depreciation	23,549,010	2,451,201	2,266,744	1,699,042	1,336,295
Utilities	22,809,177	2,024,412	3,473,847	2,339,572	1,572,713
Rent	14,975,977	491,003	9,019,992	44,964	238,568
Other	14,217,178	831,804	3,097,100	1,121,352	683,830
Equipment					
Purchases	3,095,811	144,496	0	181,191	124,568
Rentals	40,665,348	1,575,224	6,911,418	905,877	4,298,098
Depreciation	68,000,516	4,122,377	11,178,992	4,085,222	3,887,739
Repairs and Maintenance	38,997,781	2,310,667	6,299,082	2,199,042	1,348,496
Earnings-credit costs	107,709,013	6,285,764	13,328,823	8,790,331	9,581,389
Other	42,977,117	2,709,019	7,104,336	1,962,449	3,274,418
Shared costs, net	0	(3,026,998)	1,492,712	2,519,609	(1,148,176)
Recoveries	(31,379,530)	(6,460,239)	(3,283,543)	(2,165,453)	(3,014,681)
Expenses capitalized	(2,484,527)	(107,054)	(5,734)	(55,564)	(234,019)
Total	**1,268,997,855**	**74,927,816**	**236,348,411**	**73,788,206**	**78,094,973**
Reimbursements	(112,130,141)	(5,318,162)	(23,720,410)	(13,028,800)	(7,215,209)
Net expenses	1,156,867,714	69,609,654	212,628,001	60,759,406	70,879,764

REF: 73rd Annual Report of: Board of Governors of the Federal Reserve System-1986, pg. 234

EXHIBIT 3

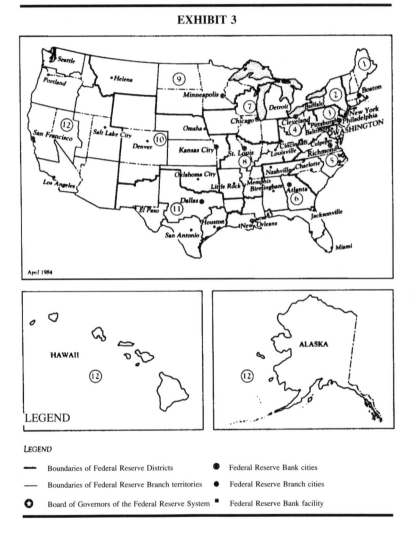

April 1984

LEGEND

▬	Boundaries of Federal Reserve Districts	●	Federal Reserve Bank cities
—	Boundaries of Federal Reserve Branch territories	●	Federal Reserve Branch cities
✪	Board of Governors of the Federal Reserve System	▪	Federal Reserve Bank facility

Richmond, Atlanta, Chicago, St. Louis, Dallas, Kansas City, Minneapolis, or San Francisco—you will find the Federal Reserve banks listed with the private banks, not with other governmental agencies.

Numerous citations, both from the courts[7] and from congressional committees, repeatedly emphasize that "the Federal Reserve banks are not a public instrument."[8] The House Committee on Banking found that "the hard truth is that the administration cannot change Federal Reserve policy."[9]

Federal Reserve banks are not only privately owned but their policies cannot be changed by the president or by the Congress. This is further evidence that the Fed is an autonomous entity, a hybrid creation of Congress that is not under the jurisdictional umbrella of the Congress or the president. In fact, in a statement in *The Computer World* of July 16, 1979, the Federal Reserve Bank of San Francisco boldly stated, "Some people still think we are a branch of the government. We are not. We are the commercial bankers' bank."[10]

"Although a creature of Congress, the Federal Reserve is, in practice, independent of that body in its policy making."[11] It neither seeks nor requires the approval of any branch of the government for its policies. The system itself decides the direction of its policies and takes whatever action it deems necessary to achieve full employment, price stability, and economic growth.

Money is the lifeblood of commerce and industry. Given this understanding, it logically follows that whoever creates and controls the money of a nation has a most awesome power. The inescapable conclusion is that the money creators can dictate the direction of governments and civilizations. In our system, this power is in the hands of a few private citizens who own the Federal Reserve banks, the commercial banks, and the thrifts.

Those not convinced by the evidence might correctly point out that it is not significant that Federal Reserve banks are private corporations since they are supervised by a governmental body, the Federal Reserve Board. It is true that the board members are appointed by the president of the United States, but it is not widely known that the board receives no appropriations from Congress. All expenses of the board are paid for by the Federal Reserve banks.

The Federal Reserve Bank of New York's publication states, "After the Fed pays the expenses of the Federal Reserve banks and the Board of Governors, it maintains a small surplus that pays the six-percent statutory dividend on the Reserve bank stock held by member banks."[12] The president, then, may name the board, but their salaries are provided for by the Federal Reserve System. It is thus probably safe to assume that the board members' allegiance is to the organization that provides those salaries.

Members of the Board of Governors of the Federal Reserve are not employees of the government; they are beings from a netherworld of politics thrust into a private corporation whose awesome task is to create and control the money supply of the United States. They are part of a private banking system that, just like the other banks in this country, is privately owned by its stockholders.

Money as Debt

Examine one of the dollar bills we use for money. At the top are the words, "Federal Reserve Note." A note is a banking IOU, a debt. But to whom is this debt owed? Each of these Federal Reserve notes is a debt to the Federal Reserve banks. Consequently, the American government (or the public, since "we the people" are the government) is head-over-heels in debt to the Federal Reserve banks.

Some people still believe that our American dollar is backed by gold and that one can go to the national Treasury or a Federal Reserve bank and redeem it for such. This is not the case. Our dollar is backed by nothing but the vitality of the American economy and has not been backed by gold since 1968. "The dollar is based on credit, and every dollar in existence represents a dollar of debt owed by an individual, a business firm, or a governmental unit."[13]

"Few understand that all our money arises out of debt and IOU operations," states Paul A. Samuelson, MIT economist.[14]

Since money is only created as debt by borrowing it with interest from the money creators, is it possible to repay the total debt (borrowed principal plus interest)? From where will the interest owed on the debt come? This question may seem simple at first, but it is, in fact, a mind-boggling one.

I asked the head of the Department of Economics and Finance at a major southern university this question while at dinner a short time ago. I posed the question at the beginning of dinner, and it remained unanswered when we finished. The professor at first thought it was a trick question, but I assured him it was not. He was perplexed. An attorney friend sat between us, along with another friend who is a certified public accountant. I had already explained the impossibility of the problem to them, so they smiled knowingly.

Before we completed the meal, I said to the professor, "Please watch my hands carefully. There is no sleight of hand involved in what I am about to demonstrate." He stared questioningly as I picked up a glass that was half full of water. Turning to him, I said, "Professor, this glass contains two ounces of water that represents all the water in existence in the world. I am now going to pour it into this empty glass I am holding in my other hand." He watched as I slowly poured the water from one glass to the other.

I passed the glass with the water to the professor. "Pour three ounces of water out of the glass I've just handed to

you. Remember, professor, there is no other water in existence on this planet." Puzzled and silent, he stared at the
glass. Then he said, "But Dr. Jaikaran, you have only poured
two ounces of water into this glass, and it is physically
impossible for me to pour out three ounces." I smiled,
"You've got it, professor." A light came into his eyes, and
he smiled. It was as if he had discovered a new scientific
truth.

"If all the money in the United States is created out of
thin air as a debt, then I see your point," he said. He continued, "The money creators, the Federal Reserve banks, the
commercial banks, and the thrifts, create money that they
lend to the government or to the private sector. The government and the private sector spend this money into circulation. It then follows that if a few people are able to repay
their debts, the interest amounts they have to pay back on
their debts must come from what someone else in the economic chain has borrowed. Somewhere along the line, a few
or many must fail, because it is impossible for all borrowers
to repay their debts. Isn't that so?" he ended.

"You are absolutely correct, professor; you have it fig-
ured out. However, let me be fair and say that there is a
small amount of debt-free money spent directly into circulation by the Federal Reserve banks," I stated.

A confused look crossed his face. "Do you mean the
Federal Reserve banks create money out of thin air and
spend it directly for their expenditures when the government, who is the sovereign authority in this country, cannot
do the same?"

"That is absolutely correct," I assured him. "That is how
it is in the United States of America." Interested now, he
leaned forward, "How do the Federal Reserve banks spend
debt-free money into circulation?"

I cited a passage from *Modern Money Mechanics*, published by the Federal Reserve Bank of Chicago. " 'The Fed does spend a rather small amount which it creates when it writes checks against no funds to pay for such things as employee salaries, real estate taxes, computer paper and landscaping.'[15] When the Federal Reserve banks spend money in this fashion, they are *spending* money into circulation as opposed to *lending* money into circulation. Money created out of thin air with the stroke of a pen or computer key and *spent* into circulation is debt free, whereas money created and *lent* into circulation is debt-money and has to be repaid, usually with interest," I explained. The professor nodded with understanding.

We now have a broader understanding of what money is and its debt character. Continuing the water metaphor, we might ask, "Is money like water on our planet, a creation of nature? Also like water, is there a finite supply that is simply recycled?"

Of course not! Money is a product of man and requires no special natural resources to create. It is created in finite amounts as debt, depending on the requirements of society. This finite quantity can only be increased by additional debt or a direct debt-free expenditure by the money creators. This finite amount can also be decreased by repayment of a debt to the money creators. The total created debt-money in circulation is *always* finite.

Chapter 3

The U.S. Dollar:
U.S. Government—Largest
Spender in the World

The greatest monopoly in this country is the Money Monopoly. As long as it exists, true freedom, and the divine right to fully enjoy the fruits of one's labors will be non-existent.

Uncle Sam is not only the largest spender on the face of the earth, with annual expenditures in excess of $1 trillion, but it is also the largest borrower—our current public debt is in excess of $3 trillion and mounting daily. Whenever government expenditures are greater than tax revenues, the government borrows money for its operations. It is simpy not true that the government creates the money it needs for its expenditures. If it could create the money it needed, then the government would not be in debt, no tax revenues would be necessary, and you and I would not have to suffer income taxes that are levied to finance governmental expenditures.

Remember, money is not only coin and currency but is also checkbook money. Almost all money in existence in the economy represents debt. Checkbook money exists only as a bookkeeping entry on the ledgers of banks and is created every time a bank makes a loan or an investment.

Let's see how the process works. As an example, assume the government needs $1 billion above and beyond its tax revenues. The money is needed for a public highway project in a particular state during a particular year. A billion dollars is a lot of money. If you converted $1 billion into $1 bills and linked them end to end, the chain of money would encircle the earth precisely 3.7 times!

Assume the Treasury receives permission from the Congress to borrow $1 billion for this public highway project. The Treasury issues bonds totaling $1 billion. Note that these bonds represent debt, so interest must be paid on them.

The Treasury bonds are then taken to the Federal Reserve. The Fed buys the bonds by increasing the Treasury's checking account at the Federal Reserve by $1 billion. This is only a bookkeeping entry. No cash changes hands. With the stroke of a pen, the Federal Reserve created $1 billion of checkbook money in the Treasury's checking account. Ultimately, American taxpayers are obligated to repay this debt with interest.

One may wonder why the Federal Reserve isn't obligated to have cash in their various banks before they write checks to the U.S. government, or to anyone else for that matter. In 1964, the Committee on Banking and Currency of the U.S. House of Representatives wrote in their publication *Money Facts* that the Federal Reserve creates money.

When the Federal Reserve writes a check, it is creating money. This can result in an increase in bank reserves—demand deposits—or in cash. If the customer prefers cash, he can request Federal Reserve notes and the Federal Reserve will have the Treasury Department print them. The Federal Reserve is a complete moneymaking machine and can issue money or checks. Unlike you and me, it never worries about "bouncing" a check because it can call up the Treasury Department's Bureau of Engraving and have them print enough $5 and $10 bills to make the check good.[1]

Who gave the Federal Reserve this awesome power, the power to create the money necessary to cover its checks? Congress "gave" the Federal Reserve the right to create money when it created the Federal Reserve System.[2] The U.S. Constitution grants the right to create money for the republic to the Congress, and only Congress can delegate this power. Actually, the Federal Reserve and the banking system simply assumed control of the money creation process in the United States, silently and without portfolio, after the Federal Reserve Act was enacted in 1913.

Congress still has the right to create money. Article 1, Section 8, Clause 5 *of the Constitution reads, "The Congress shall have the power to coin money (and) regulate the value thereof."*

This article of the Constitution was never amended, and therefore, it remains the highest law of the land. Why, then, doesn't the Congress create money for governmental expenditures debt free? It is because of a lack of knowledge of the system. Our congresspersons, like most people, still think it is the government that creates money in the United States.

Let us return to the example of the highway project. By a bookkeeping entry, $1 billion was created in the national Treasury's checking account held at a Federal Reserve bank. The next step unfolds when the Treasury begins to write checks against the $1 billion posted to its checking account. Checks are written to meet Treasury obligations for such items as defense, highway and bridge maintenance, public parks, and social services.

Those who receive these government checks deposit them in their accounts at community commercial banks. For instance, a highway contractor receives a one thousand dollar check for providing highway services to the government and deposits it in an account at Shadyside Bank, his community bank. This check is then sent to the regional Federal Reserve bank after it has been endorsed by Shadyside Bank where it was deposited. Remember, there are twelve regional Federal Reserve banks, and these have branches.

The check is cleared by the regional Federal Reserve bank where all regional community banks, like Shadyside, have checking accounts. These accounts are called reserve accounts. When the Federal Reserve bank clears the check it received from Shadyside Bank, it increases Shadyside's reserve account by one thousand dollars. This reserve account that Shadyside has at its regional Federal Reserve bank is the base used by Shadyside to create new loans in the form of checkbook money. This is not lawful money, which in America is Federal Reserve notes and coins only, but rather, this is bank-created money. It is in this fashion that all commercial banks and thrift institutions create checkbook money—unlawful money. Shadyside Bank can also convert this checkbook money into cash by exchanging it at its regional Federal Reserve bank. So, a one thousand dollar check from the Treasury drawn on an account at a Federal Reserve bank becomes two thousand dollars the very first time it is cleared by a regional Federal Reserve bank; one thousand dollars in the contractor's account and one thousand dollars in Shadyside's reserve account at its regional Federal Reserve bank. This one thousand dollars addition to Shadyside's reserve account is a free gift to Shadyside by its regional Federal Reserve bank. Such free gifts are also provided when the Federal Open Market Committee buys government securities in the open market.

EXHIBIT 4

When banks and thrifts lend, they create new checkbook money by adding funds to borrowers' checking accounts. Since commercial banks create more than three-quarters of new checkbook money, they play a special role in our financial system.

Federal Reserve Bank of New York, Public Information Department, 1985

Prior to 1980, before passage of the Depository Institutions Deregulation and Monetary Control Act, banks outside the Federal Reserve could not create money. With passage of this key act, not only commercial banks but also the thrift institutions create checkbook money when they make loans or investments (Exhibit 4).

Money Creation by Banks and Thrifts

Before banks can begin creating money, they must hold a reserve account with a regional Federal Reserve bank. Such reserve accounts are the liabilities of the Federal Reserve banks. The publication *Money Mechanics* explains, "The essential point, from the standpoint of money creation, however, is that the reserves of banks—for the most part— are liabilities of the Federal Reserve banks."[3] Clearly the quantity of reserves is totally and absolutely controlled by the Federal Reserve banks and no one else.

The mechanism used by commercial banks to create money is called "fractional reserve deposit expansion." In layman's terms, each time a bank makes a loan, it is creating new money. Banks, using this expansion process, create checkbook money many times in excess of the actual cash they have on deposit in their vaults. They enter this created money on their books as *demand deposits*.

It is easier to comprehend how this fractional reserve deposit expansion mechanism works by examining just how a bank makes a loan.

Assume a storekeeper wants to expand his business. He goes to the bank and secures a $10,000 loan. When the bank gives the storekeeper the loan, it does not hand over one thousand bills worth $10 each. Instead, the bank makes a bookkeeping entry that increases the storekeeper's checking account by $10,000. There is no transfer of funds from one account at the bank into the storekeeper's account. The bank actually *creates* new money by making the $10,000 loan. In addition, the bank expects the storekeeper to repay the loan with interest on the money it created by the bookkeeping entry.

Banking is the only business where all the inventory, like the money borrowed by the storekeeper, is created as it is needed at no cost and essentially without labor. There are no purchases made and no effort expended other than that made by the employee who entered the new numbers (merchandise)—*the checkbook money.*

Depositing into the borrower's checking account an amount equal to the amount of the loan is the way banks generally extend credit and at the same time create new money. These deposits, in short, are additions to the money supply—the M1.[4] The money supply includes a full range of monetary aggregates: M1, M2, M3, and L. M1 currently includes currency held by the nonbank public, travelers' checks from nonbank issuers, demand deposits net of cash items in process of collection and interbank balances, NOW accounts, ATS accounts, and credit union share draft balances. M2 is M1 plus overnight repurchase agreements and overnight Eurodollars, general purpose and broker/dealer money market mutual fund balances, money market deposit account balances, savings deposits, and small time deposits. M3 is M2 plus large time deposits, term RPs, term Eurodollars, and institution-only money market mutual fund balances. L is M3 plus nonbank public holdings of U.S. Savings Bonds, short-term Treasury securities, commercial papers, and bankers acceptances net of money market mutual fund holdings of these assets. The monetary base is made up of total reserve deposits with the Fed plus currency in circulation. For all intents and purposes, the only significant portion of the money supply is the M1—transaction money.

What happens when the loan is repaid? Bank credit is not a one-way street. It adds to our money supply to be sure, but our money supply declines as bank loans are repaid. Banks can destroy money as well as create it.[5] But only the principal is destroyed. The interest that is paid back to the bank is entered into their books as interest or earned income.

Assume the storekeeper obtained his loan from the Eastside Bank and used it to buy lumber. The lumber merchant deposited the proceeds from the sale in the Westside Bank. Given a 10 percent reserve requirement, the Westside Bank now lends $9,000 to Jake the plumber. Added to Jake's checking account is $9,000. Jake can now draw on this account for pipe and wrenches. This $9,000 was not transferred from any other account in the bank. The lumber merchant still has $10,000 in his account paid to him by our original storekeeper. Spurning pipe and wrenches, Jake writes out a check to Lucky's Truck Lot, and Lucky promptly deposits the $9,000 he received from Jake to his account, which is at the Southside Bank.

Southside now adds $9,000 in deposits, retains a reserve of 10 percent and has $8,100 to lend to Jane's Beauty School . . . and the process goes on. The original $10,000 deposit can expand to $100,000, with every bank honoring the 10 percent reserve requirement. Depending on reserve requirements, banks can create more money or less money. For instance, if the reserve requirement is only 5 percent, then a $10,000 deposit will be used by the banking system to expand the money supply—M1—to $200,000. The process would thus create $190,000 of new checkbook money on which banks collect interest.

On the other hand, if the reserve requirement is 20 percent, then a bank deposit of $10,000 could be used by the banking system to expand the M1 only five times as much, creating $40,000 of new checkbook money. Reserve requirements are thus very important, and they are set by the Federal Reserve banks, which, of course, are owned by the privately owned member banks. This system is akin to letting the cat guard the milk.

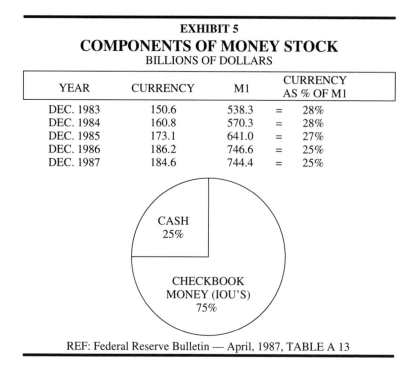

EXHIBIT 5

COMPONENTS OF MONEY STOCK
BILLIONS OF DOLLARS

YEAR	CURRENCY	M1	CURRENCY AS % OF M1	
DEC. 1983	150.6	538.3	=	28%
DEC. 1984	160.8	570.3	=	28%
DEC. 1985	173.1	641.0	=	27%
DEC. 1986	186.2	746.6	=	25%
DEC. 1987	184.6	744.4	=	25%

CASH 25%

CHECKBOOK MONEY (IOU'S) 75%

REF: Federal Reserve Bulletin — April, 1987, TABLE A 13

The Money Supply

In formulating monetary policy, the Federal Reserve has used several measures of the money supply that correspond to different concepts of money. Since one of money's traditional roles is as a medium of exchange, that is, as a means of making payments, then one of these measures consists of the things that people generally accept in payment. Hence, one measure of the nation's money supply is a total of the public's holdings of currency and deposits on which checks can be written, including traveler's checks. This measure is called the M1, and is often referred to as a transaction definition of money.[6]

M1, then, is the lifeblood of commerce and industry. It includes that segment of the total money supply that is liquid and ready for immediate use in transactions. One can use a check to buy a car, a house, or groceries. One cannot take a savings passbook, a certificate of deposit (CD), or a savings bond to buy food in a supermarket. One can use cash, checks, credit cards, and travelers' checks to make purchases, all of which are included in the definition of M1. Whenever economists refer to the "money supply," they are, in fact, referring to the M1, the transaction definition of money.

Open Market Operations

Three dozen major securities dealers provide the conduit through which the Federal Reserve engages in its open market trading operations. The Fed holds a large portfolio of government securities. If the Fed wishes to contract or restrain the growth of the money supply, it sells U.S. government securities (bonds) on the open market. Securities dealers then pay the Fed from deposits held at their local banks, and the Fed deducts an equivalent amount from the local commercial banks' reserve accounts at the various Federal Reserve banks.

As a result of this action, banks have fewer lendable funds. They are not able to make as many loans as they had been prior to the sale of the government securities. If the contraction is of sufficient magnitude, some of the banks may be forced into selling some of their investments to create a cash pool. This action could lead to a contraction throughout the banking system, and the amount of checking account money declines.

In other words, when commercial banks buy securities from the Federal Reserve, they pay with their reserves at Federal Reserve banks. This loss of reserves reduces the commercial banks' ability to create new checkbook money as new loans.

If the Fed wants to increase the money supply, it reverses the procedure and buys U.S. government securities in the open market. It then credits the reserve accounts of the banks in which securities dealers keep their money. This action increases the reserve accounts. The end result is that banks can create more checkbook money as loans. When the Federal Open Market Committee buys securities in the open market, then, it creates additional reserves as free gifts to commercial banks for loan purposes and, hence, new checkbook money.

The Federal Reserve can boost the money supply by purchasing government securities, thereby creating claims against itself. As the nation's "central" bank, the Federal Reserve is a depository for other banks in the United States, but the Fed has no bank depository of its own. A check written by the Federal Reserve, or as is often the case a credit to a seller, is deposited or credited to the account of one bank but is not deducted from the account of another bank. Likewise, when the Federal Reserve sells government securities, the payment for these securities is subtracted from the reserve account of one bank but is not added to the reserve account of another bank.

When the Fed purchases government securities, this process, by the mechanism of bookkeeping entries, puts new money back into the banking system—money that can lead to the creation of even more new money. When the Fed sells government securities, it removes money from the banking system. This, in turn, leads to further reductions in the money supply because of the system-wide Federal Reserve deposit contraction.

Monetary Policy in the United States, published by the Federal Reserve Bank of San Francisco, states, "The Federal Reserve is structured to be self-sufficient in the sense that it meets its operating expenses primarily from the interest earnings on its portfolio of securities."[7] But if the Federal Reserve has the ability to create money out of thin air, then why does it charge interest on its portfolio of government securities to produce earnings? Why does it need to make astronomical profits if it can write checks against no funds?

Chapter 4

The Planet "Doom" Experiment

By a continuing process of inflation, governments can confiscate, secretly and unobserved, an important part of the wealth of their citizens. There is no subtler, more sure way of overturning the existing basis of society than to debauch the currency. The process engages all the hidden forces of economic law on the side of destruction, and does it in a manner in which not one man in a million is able to diagnose.

—John Maynard Keynes

Keynes erroneously blamed governments for the cause of inflation because he wrongly believed that money was created by governments and was spent into circulation to finance public expenditures. But we now understand that it is not government but the privately owned Federal Reserve banks, commercial banks, and thrift institutions that create money in America.

Almost all the money circulating in the U.S. monetary system is created as debt. It is created out of thin air with

52

simple bookkeeping entries by banks, and then it is loaned into circulation either to the government or to the private sector. The monumental problem comes because only the principal is created and lent—not the interest. Still, the interest must be repaid along with the principal to the money creators, obviously a physical and mathematical impossibility. After all, if one pours a pint of water into an empty container, it would be impossible to pour out more than a pint without first adding more water to the container. Yet our monetary system demands just such an impossibility, and when some borrowers can't accomplish this impossible task, the banks that loaned only a figment of one's imagination confiscate the hard-earned tangible wealth of borrowers through foreclosures. Such acts are pernicious and totally unfair.

To understand the staggering implications of the all-debt or debt-dominant money system, one needs to conduct a controlled, scientific experiment. Before we conduct this experiment, however, it is useful to reiterate the functions of money in a free society:

to activate the production of goods and services;

to facilitate and simplify the exchange of goods and services;

to provide a relatively stable unit of measurement for the value of goods and services; and,

to provide a means of storing values or savings; namely, to enable one to convert tangible wealth into money, store this money in a bank, and convert it back to tangible wealth at a later time.

Assume that there exists another planet like Earth in another solar system. It is a fertile planet like Earth; it has natural resources; it has a sun, moon, water, vegetation, animals, and minerals. The only things missing from our hypothetical planet are human beings and tangible wealth. We'll call the planet "Doom."

To colonize this remote planet, let us assume we transport a group of hard-working, highly motivated, successful people from the planet Earth to a fertile island on Doom. They have the skills to produce all the wealth they want. They produce houses, boats, fishing nets, and tools by utilizing the natural resources, which are abundant.

Each family pursues different skills, but each has need of the skills developed by the other members of the group. They begin a barter system to trade things they need among themselves. Time passes, and this system works. They are able to barter their goods and services without a great deal of trouble.

The population begins to grow on this fertile planet, and society becomes more complex. Their economy also becomes more complex. The barter system begins to break down, and these successful, productive people see the need for a uniform medium of exchange on their planet.

The heads of the households on the planet get together and collectively decide what they are going to use as their medium of exchange. They decide they will use little pieces of paper, which will be made in the shape of triangles. Naturally these are called Doom dollars. Since these people came from Earth, they pattern their monetary system after the monetary system on Earth. They elect to use an all-debt or debt-dominant money system. Someone, therefore, has to create money, and from among their number they elect a private banker. He will create, issue, and control all the

EXHIBIT 6
ISLAND ON PLANET "DOOM"

money on the planet, exactly as the private banks do on Earth.

A farmer goes to the Doom Bank to borrow one thousand Doom dollars. The privately owned bank, like the Federal Reserve on Earth, authorizes a printer to print one thousand triangular Doom dollars and passes them over to the farmer. To get the loan, the farmer uses his farm as collateral. He also signs an agreement with the bank to repay the loan at the end of the year with 10 percent interest.

The farmer goes about his business and spends the $1,000 he borrowed on items he needs to produce various farm products. At the end of the year, the banker sends a "friendly" reminder to the farmer informing him that his debt is due. Let's assume that no one else borrows any money from the banker during the course of the year. Only $1,000 is circulating in the economy, which the farmer borrowed and spent. Will it now be possible for the farmer to repay his total debt to the bank? Obviously not, because his total debt at the end of the year is $1,000 of borrowed principal plus 10 percent interest, or a total of $1,100. But there is only $1,000 in circulation in the Doom economy.

At this point, one might question the role of the velocity of money. The formula that introduces velocity is

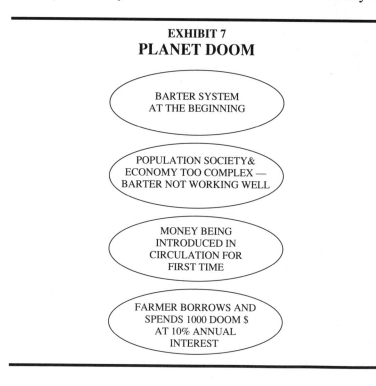

EXHIBIT 7

PLANET DOOM

BARTER SYSTEM
AT THE BEGINNING

POPULATION SOCIETY&
ECONOMY TOO COMPLEX —
BARTER NOT WORKING WELL

MONEY BEING
INTRODUCED IN
CIRCULATION FOR
FIRST TIME

FARMER BORROWS AND
SPENDS 1000 DOOM $
AT 10% ANNUAL
INTEREST

MV = PQ—the linchpin of current ecomonic theory. M is the money supply in the economy, V is the number of times during the course of one year that one dollar is spent, P is the price of goods and services, and Q is the gross national product (GNP). This formula equates the production of goods and services with the exchange of such goods and services for one year, totally ignoring all the other assets in the country that do not change hands yet have a price tag.

Does determining the velocity of money have any value? Let us assume that the farmer spent the $1000 ten times over during the course of one year and built ten storage barns, each costing $1000. Although it is true that the $1000 increased the farmer's tangible assets—storage barns—tenfold during the year, with the velocity of money being ten, at the end of the year there will still be only $1000 circulating in the economy.

Money cannot reproduce itself, therfore the velocity of money will not increase the volume or quantity of money. The velocity of money will increase the GNP, but it cannot increase the quantity of money. This simple concept seems to elude the minds of the great economists of the world.

Velocity of money cannot solve the impossible mathematical demands of an all-debt money system. In the forementioned example, the farmer will still be short the $100 interest payment he needs to repay his loan at the end of the year—no matter how many tangible assets he accrues during the course of the year. With this in mind, the concept of the velocity of money can finally be put to rest.

At this elementary level, it becomes clear that it is impossible for our farmer to repay the debt he owes. *Money is barren and cannot be expected to reproduce.* It is impossible for the farmer to repay the debt because only the principal of $1,000 was created and loaned. The interest amount that needs to be repaid along with the loan was never created or brought into circulation.

At this stage, what options does the farmer have? He can go to the friendly Doom banker and offer to pay only the interest. If the farmer pays his interest "debt" of $100 to the bank, the volume (quantity) of money left in circulation at the end of the first year—the M1—will be $900.The debt to the banker, however, still remains at $1,000—the original debt.

Since $100 is removed from the economy and paid to the banker as the 10 percent interest charge on the loan, the M1 is reduced by $100. As a consequence, the price of *existing* goods and services increases.

Why does the price of goods and services increase? Interest payments are business expenses and, as such, are "costs of doing business." These costs are passed along to consumers as a part of the price structure of existing goods and services. The $100 that was removed from the M1 as interest payment does not produce any new goods or services in the economy. It is a cost of doing business. Any expense required to do business is passed along in the price structure of existing goods and services. Despite the fact that there is a reduction in the money supply—the M1 is $900— our Doom brother is now experiencing price inflation in the marketplace. *Nonproductive interest payments on commercial loans is the major cause of price inflation.*

At the end of the second year, if the farmer again pays only the interest to the bank, the money supply decreases further. Each time an interest payment on a commercial loan is made to the bank, prices for existing goods and services increase. Again, interest payments do not go toward the production of any new goods or services, but they decrease the M1. And, because they add to the price of doing business, they get passed on—hence, inflation.

For the purpose of our experiment, we will assume that there were no more loans made by the bank. By the start of the fourth year, if this trend continues, the M1 will have decreased by 30 percent. At the beginning of the fifth year, the money supply has decreased by 40 percent. The price of goods and services will still be increasing because interest is nonproductive and, as a business expense, it is passed on to the consumer. This trend continues because there is a shortage of *debt-free* money needed to compensate for the continuous withdrawal of interest payments, "better called usury," and thus prevents a decline in the M1.

Since money is also necessary to simplify the exchange of goods and services, the shortage that occurs in the M1 by the start of the fifth year also leads to a decrease in the rate of transfer of goods and services between producers and consumers. When there is a shortage of money in the economy (a decline in the M1), relative to the quantity of goods and services, businesses fail and unemployment rises because there is less money in the hands of consumers, who cannot afford to buy as much as they want; hence, *there is a contraction in demand.* Inventories held by producers rise. An economic domino effect occurs. In other words, this continuous withdrawal of money from the system to pay interest first causes inflation of prices, and then, after a certain point is reached, a recession occurs. Bankruptcies, business failures, and unemployment increase because money that is needed for the production of goods and services and for the exchange of goods and services is in short supply.

Examine Exhibit 8. Assuming there is only one borrower on Doom, there will be absolutely no more money in circulation by the start of the eleventh year. The banker will be forced to foreclose on the farm, and the farmer will be driven into bankruptcy no matter how many assets he has.

EXHIBIT 8
FIRST OPTION-PAY INTEREST ONLY ANNUALLY

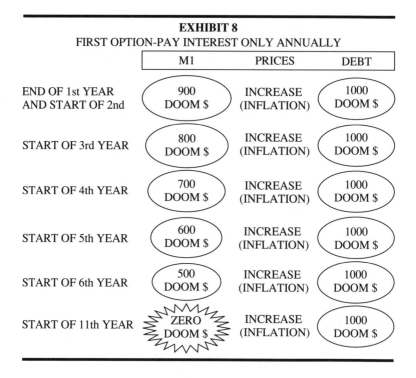

	M1	PRICES	DEBT
END OF 1st YEAR AND START OF 2nd	900 DOOM $	INCREASE (INFLATION)	1000 DOOM $
START OF 3rd YEAR	800 DOOM $	INCREASE (INFLATION)	1000 DOOM $
START OF 4th YEAR	700 DOOM $	INCREASE (INFLATION)	1000 DOOM $
START OF 5th YEAR	600 DOOM $	INCREASE (INFLATION)	1000 DOOM $
START OF 6th YEAR	500 DOOM $	INCREASE (INFLATION)	1000 DOOM $
START OF 11th YEAR	ZERO DOOM $	INCREASE (INFLATION)	1000 DOOM $

The banker can actually foreclose on the farmer at the end of the first year, since it will be impossible for the farmer to repay the total debt of $1,100. By allowing the farmer to pay only interest at the end of every year, the banker is only postponing the eventual bankruptcy and fore-closure until an economic recession or depression occurs or until no more money remains in circulation.

There is a second option, but this option again represents only a postponement of the inevitable catastrophe of bank-ruptcy and foreclosure. Since Doom is new to commerce, let's assume the farmer decides to maintain his original borrowed principal in circulation. At the end of every year he makes a deal with the banker to borrow the interest that has accrued during the year, which, of course, never leaves the bank. He maintains the M1 at a stable level but increases the magnitude of his debt on the banker's ledger by borrowing the interest every year.

Exhibit 9 shows that at the end of the first year the money in circulation totals $1,000; however, the debt owed by the farmer is $1,100. If the farmer borrows the interest on an annual basis, the debt will be compounded annually. Exhibit 9 demonstrates the growth of the farmer's debt at the rate of 10 percent compounded annually. At the end of the ninth year, the accumulated interest of $1,144 will be greater than all the money in circulation, namely $1,000. At this stage, financial collapse results. Dollars that do not exist cannot be used to make interest payments. The banker, knowing that the annual interest payment is greater than all the money in circulation, would be foolhardy to extend any additional credit!

Table 4 shows the growth of a debt of $1,000 at an annual 10 percent compound interest rate, maintaining $1,000 in circulation. By the end of the seventieth year, the interest on the $1,000 original debt is $788,921. Keep in mind that the money to cover the interest amount does not exist, so it is impossible for the total debt to be repaid. Yet, all the efforts of the most learned economists who advise our government are directed toward this impossibility.

If there are more participants in the borrowing process, the outcome will be different! Suppose we have farmer A and shopkeeper B, each borrowing $1,000 from the Doom banker and spending this money into the economy. Everything moves along smoothly, and at the end of the first year, the "friendly" banker informs both the farmer and shop-

Debt Virus

EXHIBIT 9
SECOND OPTION — MAINTAIN $1000 CONSTANT AND BORROW
INTEREST ON EXISTING DEBT ANNUALLY
GROWTH OF $1000 DEBT AT 10% ANNUAL COMPOUND INTEREST

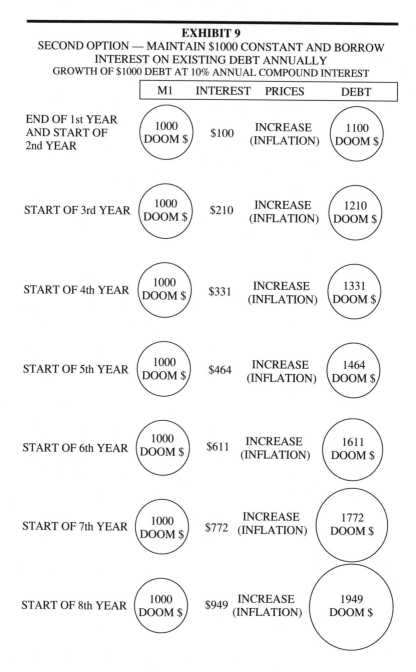

	M1	INTEREST	PRICES	DEBT
END OF 1st YEAR AND START OF 2nd YEAR	1000 DOOM $	$100	INCREASE (INFLATION)	1100 DOOM $
START OF 3rd YEAR	1000 DOOM $	$210	INCREASE (INFLATION)	1210 DOOM $
START OF 4th YEAR	1000 DOOM $	$331	INCREASE (INFLATION)	1331 DOOM $
START OF 5th YEAR	1000 DOOM $	$464	INCREASE (INFLATION)	1464 DOOM $
START OF 6th YEAR	1000 DOOM $	$611	INCREASE (INFLATION)	1611 DOOM $
START OF 7th YEAR	1000 DOOM $	$772	INCREASE (INFLATION)	1772 DOOM $
START OF 8th YEAR	1000 DOOM $	$949	INCREASE (INFLATION)	1949 DOOM $

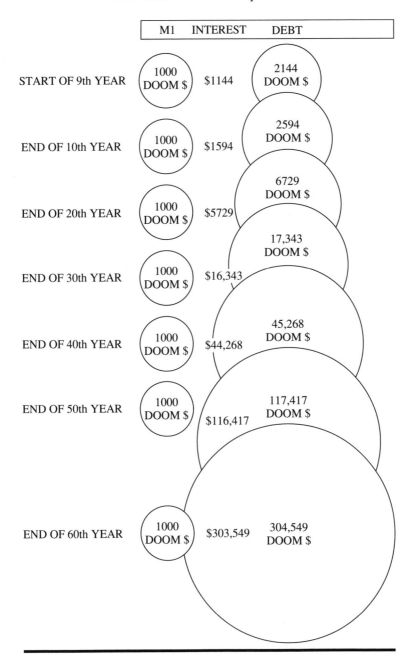

M1	INTEREST	DEBT

START OF 9th YEAR — 1000 DOOM $ | $1144 | 2144 DOOM $

END OF 10th YEAR — 1000 DOOM $ | $1594 | 2594 DOOM $

END OF 20th YEAR — 1000 DOOM $ | $5729 | 6729 DOOM $

END OF 30th YEAR — 1000 DOOM $ | $16,343 | 17,343 DOOM $

END OF 40th YEAR — 1000 DOOM $ | $44,268 | 45,268 DOOM $

END OF 50th YEAR — 1000 DOOM $ | $116,417 | 117,417 DOOM $

END OF 60th YEAR — 1000 DOOM $ | $303,549 | 304,549 DOOM $

Debt Virus

TABLE 4
GROWTH OF $1000 DEBT
TO MAINTAIN $1000 IN CIRCULATION AT 10% ANNUAL COMPOUND INTEREST

Year	Total Borrowed Principal (P)	Interest Due at Year End (at 10%) (I)	Total Debt at Year End (D)	Money in Circulation (M1)
1	$1,000	$100	$1,100	$1,000
2	1,000	210	1,210	1,000
3	1,000	331	1,331	1,000
4	1,000	464	1,464	1,000
5	1,000	611	1,611	1,000
10	1,000	1,594	2,594	1,000
20	1,000	5,729	6,729	1,000
30	1,000	16,343	17,343	1,000
40	1,000	44,268	45,268	1,000
50	1,000	116,417	117,417	1,000
60	1,000	303,549	304,549	1,000
70	1,000	788,921	789,921	1,000

keeper that their loans are due. The total sum due the banker is $2,200, assuming both borrowed at an annual interest rate of 10 percent.

In Exhibit 11, we see that, since there is only $2,000 circulating in the economy and the debt to the banker is now

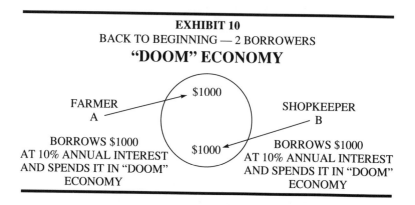

EXHIBIT 10
BACK TO BEGINNING — 2 BORROWERS
"DOOM" ECONOMY

FARMER A → $1000

SHOPKEEPER B

$1000

BORROWS $1000 AT 10% ANNUAL INTEREST AND SPENDS IT IN "DOOM" ECONOMY

BORROWS $1000 AT 10% ANNUAL INTEREST AND SPENDS IT IN "DOOM" ECONOMY

EXHIBIT 11
2 BORROWERS, (continued)

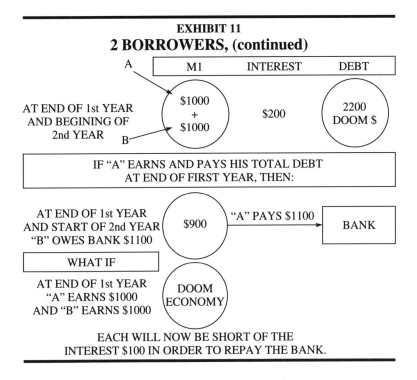

A	M1	INTEREST	DEBT

AT END OF 1st YEAR
AND BEGINING OF
2nd YEAR   B

$1000 + $1000

$200

2200 DOOM $

IF "A" EARNS AND PAYS HIS TOTAL DEBT
AT END OF FIRST YEAR, THEN:

AT END OF 1st YEAR
AND START OF 2nd YEAR
"B" OWES BANK $1100

$900

"A" PAYS $1100

BANK

WHAT IF

AT END OF 1st YEAR
"A" EARNS $1000
AND "B" EARNS $1000

DOOM ECONOMY

EACH WILL NOW BE SHORT OF THE
INTEREST $100 IN ORDER TO REPAY THE BANK.

$2,200, it is mathematically impossible for both A and B to repay their total debts. Only the principal was created as debt, and the interest amount due on each principal amount does not exist.

Now, if farmer A is able to repay his debt at the end of the first year, then he will remove $1,100 from the Doom economy, leaving $900. At the end of the first year, shopkeeper B will be short $200 if he wants to repay his total debt.

If A and B are extremely hard working and highly motivated and are able to earn back $1,000 each from the Doom economy, what will happen at the end of the year? They each will be short $100 to pay the Doom banker, and both will fail. In this portion of our experiment, we assume that the skills of the participants in the marketplace are evenly matched and that they each possess the ability to earn what they borrowed. They both fail because there is no money created to satisfy the interest payments required by the banker. The experiment can be expanded to include many more borrowers, but the result will still be the same. Many people operating in the marketplace will eventually suffer either bankruptcies or foreclosures. The only winner in this system is the private money creator.

Doom's system is exactly like the system operating in America today. In the all-debt or debt-dominant monetary system, for one to succeed others must fail. Failure is not necessarily caused by mismanagement or laziness. Bankruptcies, foreclosures, business failures, unemployment, and bank failures are actually built into the all-debt monetary system.

The Deadly Formula

Debt grows as money is created and lent at interest. If you graphically plot the growth of $1,000 of debt at 10 percent compound interest from Table 4, the shape of your graph will be as in Figure 3. The debt grows slowly at first, but then mushrooms. This upwardly sloping curve is a classic exponential curve. The general formula for an exponential curve is $y = a^x$. In this formula, x is the exponent. In other words, y equals a multiplied by itself x times. So, if $a = 4$ and $x = 5$, then y equals $4 \times 4 \times 4 \times 4 \times 4$ *equals 1024*. If a is a fixed value, the larger x is, the greater will be the value of y.

The compound interest formula for debt is $D = P[1+ r]^n$ (where D equals the debt, P is the debt principal, r equals the

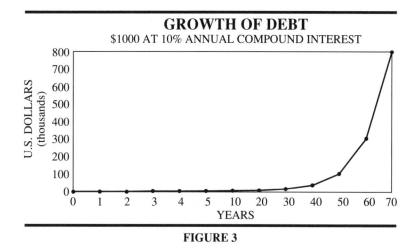

GROWTH OF DEBT
$1000 AT 10% ANNUAL COMPOUND INTEREST

FIGURE 3

rate of interest, and *n* equals the number of compounding periods, usually months or years). *This is the deadly formula,* the exponential formula in which debt becomes a function of the rate of interest and the passage of time. It is this deadly formula, employed by the present money creators, that propagates the "debt virus" that will eventually lead to worldwide poverty, disease, destruction, and death!

When Einstein was being congratulated on his great scientific discoveries, he remarked that his work did not compare with what he regarded as the greatest invention—"compound interest."[1] When Napoleon was shown an interest table, he reflected for a while and then commented, "The deadly facts herein revealed, lead me to wonder that this monster, *interest*, has not devoured the whole human race. It would have done so long ago if bankruptcy and revolutions had not acted as counter poisons."[2] Must we continue to use bankrupties and revolutions to counteract the deadly effects of escalating debt?

On the planet Doom, all money is created as debt. It is mathematically impossible to repay the total debt—principal and interest. For commerce to continue for a period, only the interest payments on the debt can be repaid or else borrowed from the money creators. This continuous removal of nonproductive interest payments or the borrowing of interest causes the prices of goods and services to increase and reduces the M1 in relation to the size of the debt.

In other words, producers will demand more Doom debt-dollars for existing goods and services because their interest payments or borrowing costs are an expense of doing business. This sequence will lead to a decrease in the purchasing power of the Doom debt-dollar.

It is important to remember that any money in the vaults of the banks is no longer part of the M1. Only checking accounts and cash in the hands of the nonbank public are considered the M1, and the M1 is the lifeblood of commerce and industry.

Since interest payments are continuously being removed from the M1, the prices of goods and services are being forced up at the same time as money in circulation is diminishing. Thus, there is a legitimate need to borrow more money from the money creators to pay interest and to maintain money in circulation to facilitate the exchange of existing goods and services (now offered at higher prices).

This increased borrowing is erroneously believed to be the cause of inflation. In actuality, inflation is primarily caused by nonproductive commercial loan interest payments to lenders, whether they are money creators or not. A detailed account of the true causes of inflation will be discussed in a later chapter.

The growth of the M1 that occurs during a period of inflation is partly due to increased borrowing by the public to pay not only their interest charges but also the interest on the borrowings of others who provide goods and services for public consumption. Because the interest payments made by other producers are included in the prices of their goods, they are passed along to the consumer in the form of increased prices for those goods. Borrowing is also necessary to maintain an adequate money supply to facilitate the exchange of existing goods and services, not necessarily to pay for the production of new goods and services.

When prices of goods and services rise, the purchasing power of money diminishes. Such a decrease in purchasing power is induced by debt. The greater the debt and the higher the interest rate, the greater the interest payments and the greater the decrease in the purchasing power of money.

Examine Exhibit 9 once again and see what happens to debt when one tries to keep $1,000 in constant circulation in the Doom economy. In the ninth year the interest is $1,144. If one assumes the initial $1,000 produced 1,000 pounds of butter, and it was initially sold at $1 per pound, then by the start of the ninth year—because of the interest costs factored into the new price—butter would cost more than $2 per pound. The price of butter has thus more than doubled, or the purchasing power of the Doom dollar decreased by more than 100 percent. The intrinsic value of the butter did not change; however, the purchasing power of the Doom dollar diminished. This diminution in the purchasing power of the Doom dollar was induced by increased debt at interest.

Inflation is correctly defined as a debt-induced decrease in the purchasing power of money. It is caused by an incremental increase in the cost of goods and services as a result of interest charges, which are business expenses.

A recession, on the other hand, is caused by an absolute shortage of money in the economy. The greater the shortage, the greater the recession. When a recession is long and pronounced, it is known as an economic depression. In an all-debt monetary system, depressions are caused by a severe and absolute shortage of cash and checkbook money in the economy.

A rise in the Consumer Price Index (CPI), inflation, economic recessions, economic depressions, and a decrease in the purchasing power of money are all results of the continual withdrawal of money from the M1 to pay nonproductive interest to the money creators. These are the symptoms. The disease is our debt-dominant money system, which has a built-in mathematical error. Correct this error and cure the disease. The symptoms will disappear.

Chapter 5

The Phoenix Response

Change is one of the constants of the universe. If we are not prepared to adapt to it, then out of necessity, we must be prepared to become extinct for the lack of it.

Suppose that out of the ashes of the failed economy on the Planet Doom rises a monetary system driven by the winds of change. In this prototype economy, the Phoenix Experiment, people who are willing and able to work hard have no limits on the amount of wealth they can accumulate other than the limits they set for themselves. They cannot fail as they do under the all-debt money system, which functions on the premise that for one to succeed in the marketplace others must fail, though not necessarily as a result of their own faults. Here, people fail if they are lazy or have no desire to succeed or if they mismanage their businesses or their households.

You will remember that on the Planet Doom a conscious decision was made to introduce money into the Doom economy for the first time. A banker was selected, and the farmer borrowed one thousand Doom dollars from him. The farmer signed a note for $1,000 at 10 percent interest compounded annually, using his farm as collateral on the $1,000 loan the bank advanced him. The farmer pursued his farming endeavors and spent the $1,000 he borrowed from the bank. Assume that no one else borrowed and spent any money. Now let's suppose that one hundred debt-free genuine Doom dollars were spent into the economy to activate the production of goods and services or to purchase existing goods and services. Debt-free dollars are those created and spent or otherwise brought into circulation by the governing authority but that do not increase debt in the money system. Remember, debt-dollars are created and lent to the economic arena and must be paid back—usually at interest.

At this point, let us not concern ourselves with the origin of this debt-free money. The important fact is that there are one hundred debt-free dollars in circulation in the Doom economy. This sum is not owed to anyone and does not have to be repaid to anyone in particular. The money supply, the M1, is now made up of the one thousand debt-dollars originally borrowed from the money creator (the banker) and of one hundred debt-free dollars, or a total of $1,100.

Theoretically, the farmer can now earn $1,100 from the economy to repay the banker, because there is $1,100 circulating in the economy. On the other hand, the farmer may not repay the total debt. He may choose to repay only the interest of $100 and keep the original principal of $1,000 in the economy to expand his business. Since the farmer still has his original one thousand debt-dollars, there is no need to pass on the $100 interest cost to the price of goods and services initially produced by the $1,000. But human behavior dictates that, since the $100 interest payment to the banker was a legitimate business expense, the farmer may pass this cost on to the consumer through the price of existing goods and services.

Beginning the second year, the M1 is one thousand debt-dollars. If the M1 again increases by one hundred debt-free dollars, the new M1 will once more be $1,100. Again, do not be concerned about the source of these debt-free dollars at this point. Theoretically, there will not be a shortage of money in the M1 to repay the total debt to the bank, assuming interest rates do not change.

In the all-debt money system demonstrated in the Doom experiment of the previous chapter, there was no debt-free money. As a result, it was impossible for the farmer to repay the aggregate debt, that is, the borrowed principal plus interest. Interest payments to banks are nonproductive. If such payments do not reduce the debt-money in circulation, there is no need to pass on the interest costs as price increases. Unfortunately, human beings always want as much as they can get for as little labor as possible, and if one wants to increase profit margins without expending more energy to produce additional goods, prices will increase, as the interest payments get passed on.

If the M1 is kept constant by annually replenishing nonproductive interest payments to banks with debt-free money equivalent to the total interest due, there will not be a shortage of money in the economy. Without a shortage of money in the economy, there will be nothing to slow down or prevent production and the transfer of goods and services between producers, retailers, and consumers. Inventories will not build up, no slowdowns in production will occur, and business failures, bankruptcies, foreclosures, and unemployment caused by a shortage of money in the marketplace will be a thing of the past. Recessions and depressions will be prevented since both of these events are caused by a shortage of debt-free money in the economy.

*One of the most monumental misconceptions of econom-
ics is that inflation is caused by too much money in relation
to goods and services in the marketplace.* Let us examine
this claim. During a recent discussion, a Ph.D. economist
claimed that, if the money suppy is doubled and products
and services remain constant, the prices of products and
services will double. Conversely, he stated that if the money
supply (M1) is halved and the quantity of products and
services remain unchanged, the prices of these products and
services will be halved.

For the foregoing assumptions to be true, the following
assumption must also be true: that at any given time in the
economic arena, the money supply equals the total prices of
all products and services. This last assumption is a fallacy;
it will be dealt with at length in Chapter 6.

Inflation is caused mainly by nonproductive interest
payments on commercial loans, which are passed on to the
prices of existing goods and services. Increased wages, which
are passed on to the cost of products and services as a
business expense, are not, however, the primary causes of
inflation. Additional reasons for inflation are higher profit
motivations, plain and simple greed, and the desire to get
something for nothing.

The money supply is deliberately contracted by the Fed
when prices rise, thus producing recessions rather than pre-
venting them. During these inflationary periods, our financial cognoscenti restrict the money supply by raising interest
rates at the Federal Reserve and commercial banks, making
borrowing more difficult at a time when the opposite course
of action is needed. This "tight money" policy leads to an
absolute decrease in the money supply—M1—and an economic slowdown becomes inevitable.

On May 4, 1990, a Houston economist—self-styled as
America's Main Street Economist—stated on National Pub-

lic Radio that the Fed should temporarily kill the economy to bring down inflation. How does one "temporarily" kill someone or something? Is there such a thing as a temporary death?

The administrations in Brazil and Poland have been employing Western economists that think just like this "Main Street Economist" to solve their current economic dilemma. On May 10, 1990, the *Wall Street Journal* reported that a catastrophic economic depression is being engineered in Brazil.

Needless to say, I was upset that our Main Street Economist was communicating false information and bad ideas. I wrote to him explaining that too much money does not cause inflation. Sure enough, he called to inform me that a recession or a depression has historically cured inflation in America and the rest of the world—it is the only way inflation has been controlled in the past.

I conceded this much to America's Main Street Economist, but I then left this question for him to ponder: "Yes, but how would you like me to treat your fingertip infection by amputating your arm at the shoulder, or would not decapitation cure your headache?"

It is true that recessions have historically been used to treat inflation, but only at an extreme price to the productive elements of society. During recessions, the productive elements are dispossessed of their wealth through bankruptcies, business failures, and unemployment. Headaches and fingertip infections can be treated by much less drastic means than decapitation and amputation respectively. Similarly, inflation can be treated by means other than economic recessions and depressions.

As long as such erroneous thinking is allowed to continue regarding the cause and effect relationships inherent in the system, we will continue to experience the familiar business cycles that have plagued our economy since 1764. A period of inflationary expansion is followed by a peak, which is followed by an economic contraction, which is followed by a trough or recession, which is followed by another inflationary expansion, and on ad infinitum. Bankruptcies, foreclosures, business failures, and unemployment will continue, and the only losers will be the honest, hard-working, and productive elements of our society.

What steps can we take to remedy a situation that has been festering almost since this nation was born? Let's examine the Phoenix Experiment carefully to seek part of the answer.

What will happen if the farmer repays only the interest due to the money creator at the end of the first year and decides to pass the expense of the interest on to the consumer as part of the price for his goods, despite the fact that there were debt-free dollars circulating in the economy? True price inflation will result. But the M1, which still contains the $1,000 originally borrowed, remains the same. There is no shortage of money to exchange as producers sell their products and consumers purchase their products.

Inflation in and of itself is not bad as long as there is ample money circulating in the economy to facilitate the exchange of goods and services. As long as inflation is matched by increased amounts of money in the hands of consumers, inventories will not build up. What difference does it make if one has to pay $1 million for a car if one has $1 billion? Only when there is an inadequate amount of money in the hands of consumers do goods go unsold and inventories pile up. Manufacturers then have to reduce or stop production, and people find themselves without work.

In a sound economic system, the supply of money meets the current need for it in the marketplace. There should be a balance between the supply and the need. However, it is impossible to maintain such a balance unless the creation of money and the ability to tax it out of existence are controlled by the same entity. If these powers, the ability to create money and the ability to tax, are in different hands—one in public and one in private hands—and these two sectors are not totally accountable to each other, an imbalance occurs. This concept seems to evade our deepest economic thinkers.

One of man's greatest instincts is self-preservation; thus the private sector acts to the detriment of the public sector out of self-interest. To maintain a true balance between the supply and the need for money in the marketplace, the money creation and taxation powers must be in the same hands. This is not the case in the United States.

We now realize and understand the paramount importance of keeping a quantity of debt-free money in the economy. We can now expand the Phoenix Experiment. Would it make any difference if there are two, two hundred, two million, or two hundred million borrowers in the economic system of Phoenix? No. It makes no difference how many individual borrowers there are. What must be appreciated is that a volume of debt-free money no less than the total interest payments owed to banks should be put into the economy annually. With a fraction of the M1 being debt-free, the original borrowed principal in any given year will not be reduced when interest payments to banks are removed from the economy, provided the annual debt-free expenditure equals the annual interest payments on the total debt.

No shortage of money will thus occur. With no shortage of money in the economy, the exchange of goods and services between producers, retailers, and consumers will proceed uninterrupted. Economic growth will continue uninterrupted ad infinitum as long as there is a need for the products and services offered.

Of course, if one tries to set up a business exporting coal to Newcastle, the coal capital of England, it will fail because of demand factors. But at least in this primitive economic model it is not a requirement for some businesses to fail for others to succeed.

Eureka! To prevent the boom-bust-boom-bust economic cycles of inflation, recession, bankruptcies, business failures, unemployment, and foreclosures, a fraction of the money in circulation in the economy must be debt-free. This fraction should be at least equal to the amount being removed annually from the money supply to pay interest to banks.

Nature is wonderfully balanced, but our economic system has some maddening imbalances. Bring our system into equilibrium, and some wondrous changes will occur in the United States.

Chapter 6

The Anatomy and Physiology
of Inflation

The monetary scientist, like the philosopher and artist, seeks the truth, then makes his appeal. My task is to per- suade you to touch and feel, to look and perceive, to listen and hear, and above all, to challenge you to become aware and understand.

Current Economic Teaching

In all centers of higher economic education, inflation is defined as a general increase in prices; that is, when prices throughout the economy are, on average, rising. During periods of inflation, some prices rise faster than others, and some prices even fall—witness the prices of pocket calcula- tors, home computers, and silicon chips during the inflation- ary 1970s. On the other hand, crude oil prices rose at a rate five times faster than the average price increases between 1972 and 1981.

Perceptions of whether or not inflation is increasing at "moderate" or "rapid" rates depends on perceptions of recent trends. During the mid-1950s when prices rose at about a 2 percent rate per year, an annual inflation rate of 5 percent would have been unthinkable. In 1966 a price increase of 3.3 percent was considered so alarming that it motivated the government to impose strict anti-inflationary measures.

In the early 1980s, after several years of double-digit and near double-digit inflation, an annual rate of 5 percent would have been considered a miracle.

In countries like Brazil, Argentina, Mexico, Venezuela, and Poland—where prices have more than doubled annually in recent years—the inflation rate experienced in the United States in the 1970s and 1980s would have been welcomed. Thus, the rate of inflation, like other measures of prices, must be evaluated in relative terms.

Types of Inflation

Current economic teaching explains that a general rise in prices can occur for different reasons. Over the years, economists have defined three different types of inflation:

demand-pull inflation

cost-push inflation

structural inflation

Demand-pull inflation occurs when too many dollars chase too few goods; thus demand-pull inflation concentrates on the "too many dollars" side of the inflation equation. Conventional economists claim that demand-pull inflation occurs when the amount of money increases more rapidly than the supply of such goods and services. This excess money, the theory states, causes prices to be bid up—thus the demand "pulls" up the general level of prices.

Cost-push inflation concentrates on the "too few goods" side of the inflation equation. Cost-push inflation occurs, according to followers of this theory, when autonomous increases in production costs or disruptions in supplies cause firms to restrain their delivery of goods and services into the marketplace at prevailing prices, again, causing prices to be bid up.

As previously noted, prices are constantly changing in a dynamic economy. Some prices are rising while others are falling. When rising prices dominate, the general level of prices increases. Bottlenecks in the economy, say economists, may cause the prices of certain critical goods—steel or oil, for example, or precision drilling machines—to be bid up.

In one part of the economy, specific bottlenecks may cause certain prices to rise, while in other parts of the economy surpluses may develop. These surpluses cause some specific prices to fall, the theorists assert, and price hikes in the "bottleneck" sectors are moderated by price declines in other sectors. Thus, structural inflation occurs when prices in some areas do not fall as readily as prices rise in the "bottleneck" sector, resulting in a general upward creep in prices.

Economists on the Effects of Inflation

People are concerned about inflation out of fear that rising prices will lower their standard of living. Alarming increases in the cost of housing, food, and clothing are cited as proof that our "standard of living" is falling. Living standards are determined by the relationship between the income citizens have to spend and the prices they must pay for the items they want and need. If income is rising faster than prices, living standards are rising. If income is rising slower than prices, living standards are falling. The relationship between income and prices thus determines the direction of change in economic well-being.

Economists claim that inflation can redistribute income among members of society. They theorize that inflation redistributes wealth from lenders to borrowers when the inflation rate has not been correctly anticipated. Economists also theorize that inflation can cause a reduction in economic efficiency. Anticipated inflation can divert resources from productive to unproductive investments and thus reduce the economy's productive capacity.

Ruffin and Gregory state in *Principles of Economics* that "inflation causes cash-soaked doctors and lawyers to rush to art auctions and invest in questionable schemes to avoid the inflation tax. While the poor might be just trying to make ends meet, the rich are preoccupied in rather useless games of "musical chairs." Economists also say that inflation can cause changes in output and employment in that it can motivate producers to either produce more or less goods or motivate workers to work more or less hours.

A Monetary Scientist's Dissection of Inflation

Before we embark on this anatomical lesson, let's examine how prices are set on end products offered for sale in the marketplace as well as for goods and services. By end products, I mean clothing as an end product of the intermediate product of cotton, an automobile as the end product of the intermediate product of steel, and so on.

Most people think prices are set by calculating the total expenditures for producing the products, then dividing these costs by the number of products or services produced over a certain period of time, usually a year. The final price includes labor costs and profit for the producers.

The businessman adds in the return he expects on his investment, his "cost of capital" or his "risk premium"—that is, the compensation the businessman expects for assuming the risks of the endeavor he has chosen with all its related production costs.

More often than not, the explanation of the price determination process states that "profit" is added to the other costs to arrive at a final price. A "greed" factor is thus introduced when this profit is added without calculating capital or risk costs, or is done arbitrarily and the "profit" is in excess of the real costs, that is, tangible and capital return costs. When the profit figure includes this "greed" factor, pricing is affected, and the businessman is placed in the position of receiving something for nothing, a condition that violates basic natural and moral laws.

In fact, some natural and moral laws shed light on this matter. Sir Isaac Newton said that "for every action there is an equal and opposite reaction," and Jesus Christ said, "What we sow, so shall we reap." The first is a scientific or natural law, and the latter is a moral or spiritual law, but the idea conveyed by both statements is the same.

Put into economic terms, our returns in life or business should be in direct proportion to our efforts or our service. Anything we expect beyond our actual costs, which have been previously enumerated, involve "greed," which violates both natural and moral laws. These laws are not often articulated in connection with economic discussions, but violation of these basic laws cause a myriad of social, cultural, moral, and financial problems.

Now let us look critically at demand-pull inflation, the condition of "too many dollars chasing too few goods, . . . thus bidding up prices." Ruffin and Gregory have this to say about fiat money: *"Governments have a monopoly over the issue of fiat money,"* and, *"The most important example of fiat money in the United States is paper currency called Federal Reserve notes issued by the Federal Reserve System, rather than the United States Treasury."*

Here are two contradictory statements. The first states that government has a monopoly over the issuance of fiat money, and the second informs us that the U.S. Treasury does not issue fiat money. Such contradictions are quite commonplace in discussions of economics. But this book has already established that money in the United States— Federal Reserve notes and checkbook money—is created by the privately owned banks; namely, Federal Reserve banks, commercial banks, and thrift institutions.

Since money comes into existence as debt, the aggregate debt is mathematically unpayable since only the principal is created. It becomes mathematically impossible to repay interest on money that has been created in this fashion, since the interest was not created along with the debt. For interest to be repaid, it must be taken from another person's borrowed principal (refer to the chapter detailing the Doom Experiment).

If it is true that too much money chasing too few goods causes inflation—the demand-pull theory—traditional economists are faced with some serious questions. Governments, citizens, and economists all agree that inflation is bad. In fact, inflation hurts the productive members of society most by lowering their standard of living. Scholars of inflation also know that inflation has been around for thousands of years and was present since the ancient Egyptian civilization. And scholars know that inflation has been the primary cause of hunger and perdition for countless millions since the dawn of civilization.

But inflation has been present only in all-debt money systems. And if too much money is the cause of inflation, and if governments have a monopoly over the issuance of fiat money, an important question arises: Why do governments allow an increase in the money supply if they know that such an action will be harmful to the economy, which they are obliged to nurture? This action would make no scientific sense.

When asked to explain this contradiction, an economics professor at a major southern university laughingly stated that politicians want to be elected, so they want to keep taxes low. They keep taxes low so that the electorate will continue their tenure in office; they would rather create money than increase taxes. This same professor could not explain how this nation functioned very efficiently for over 140 years without an income tax. He was quick to say, however, that he would prefer to have his tax lowered than raised, when asked which his choice would be.

Since 1900, inflation as reflected in the decrease of the purchasing power of the dollar or Federal Reserve note has been increasing exponentially, to the point that the 1900 dollar in 1990 has a purchasing power of about six cents. In other words, prices for the same products have increased seventeen-fold since 1900.

Note that when you go to the supermarket, department store, or car dealership, salespeople hover about, trying to persuade you to part with your money and leave with their products—products that ten years ago would have required 40 percent of the current price. In reality, despite price increases due to inflationary forces, it is the product, through its producer and distributor, that chases the dollar. It is not the other way around, as most economists would have you believe.

You need only look at television, leaf through a magazine, or page through a newspaper to confirm that there are thousands of ads trying to sell you something. If the problem was too much money chasing too few goods, one might expect to see consumers—cash in hand—seeking out various products in all those ads. A more scientific explanation of inflation should be demanded.

If too much money chasing too few goods is the cause of inflation, then we must demand to know where the excess money comes from, who is getting it, and how they are getting it. If too much money causes inflation, then not only will the price of goods and services rise, but consumers will receive more money through income and wages. They will then be able to purchase the higher priced goods, because they now have more money in their pockets.

Is inflation a curse? What difference does it make if the consumer has to pay a million dollars for a car if he has a billion dollars? The only time inflation is bad is when the car costs one million dollars and the consumer does not have enough money or the ability to earn enough money to purchase it.

At an auction where there are many buyers but few products, the price is determined by the person selling the product in most cases. Unless the sale is a forced or distress sale, the seller usually attaches a minimum bid that will cover all expenditures, including his time and expertise. The seller hopes some of the previously mentioned physicians and lawyers will attend the sale, so that bidders will bid up the price of the item. Though it is true that people are bidding against each other for the product, is money the cause of the increase in price as bids come in? Or is the price a result of the opportunism of the seller, taking advantage of a special situation? In this instance, to conclude that money is causing the price to go up is like saying that the windmill causes the wind to blow.

During a recent weather disturbance in the Houston area, people rushed to the hardware stores for plywood to board up their windows and doors. As soon as the rush to get plywood started, the sellers of plywood increased their prices sixfold. The sellers' costs for the product did not increase one penny, but the merchant understood that he could raise his prices by six times and "get away with it" —a perfect example of "opportunism" (the greed factor) at work. It would be foolhardy to suggest that excess money in the buyers' pockets was the reason plywood prices rose. Prices rose as a result of the greed of the sellers, capitalizing on the shortage of plywood.

The universally accepted definition of the price of a tangible asset challenges some of the traditional economic dicta about how prices are set. The price of a tangible asset in the marketplace is defined as the price a willing buyer and a willing seller agree on.

Currently, many Third World countries and countries in the Eastern bloc are throwing off the shackles of communism and hiring Western economists to confront their economic problems. One of the measures being recommended by economists is to devalue the currency. In other words, a law is passed decreeing a devaluation of the currency by, for example, 100 percent. Consequently, just prior to imposition of the law one could buy a loaf of bread for one unit of currency. Afterward, the same loaf of bread will cost two units of currency.

The intrinsic value of the bread did not change, but the purchasing power of the money changed. With a currency devaluation, the holders of currency—the wealth-producing middle class workers with little or no property and a small amount of savings—are those who get "Scrooged."

When a devaluation of currency occurs, there is a sharp drop in purchasing power. If the devaluation is 100 percent and the total money supply in the economy is (for simplicity) $100 before the devaluation, then immediately after the devaluation the total purchasing power would halve. To restore 100 percent purchasing power after devaluation, the money supply must be doubled to $200. If the money supply is not doubled, there will not be enough money in the economy to facilitate the exchange of existing goods and services between manufacturers, retailers, and consumers. The consumers will not have enough purchasing power to buy from retailers. Goods will go unsold, inventories will pile up, manufacturers will decrease production, resulting in labor force layoffs, rising unemployment, business failures, and some bank failures.

To prevent this sequence of events, purchasing power must be restored in the marketplace. Where will the additional $100 come from? Will the government print and then spend this money into the marketplace for its expenditures? But, if governments did create money so freely, then why would they have such huge debts? Rather, the government prefers to impose taxes or borrow money to finance its debt. The money supply is increased usually by increased borrowing by government or the private sector.

But, there are two governments that create and spend money to finance their public expenditures instead of borrowing it and thus have no public debt. These are the jewels in the English Channel, Guernsey and Jersey. These two islands function with high standards of living, low taxes, low inflation, and zero unemployment. They also enjoy an extraordinary amount of common sense in the management of their money.

But now let's turn to the cost-push inflation argument, an argument that centers on the "too few goods" side of the inflation equation. This theorem states that when production costs increase for whatever reason, manufacturers decrease their offerings of goods and services to the market at prevailing prices, thus again bidding up prices. Cost-push inflation is essentially the same as demand-pull inflation, except that it is stated in reverse, and I have already dealt at length with the theory of too much money chasing too few goods as a cause of inflation.

Structural inflation addresses the bidding up of prices on certain critical goods and is no more than a variant of demand-pull and cost-push inflation under another name. The argument linking too much money and price inflation has thus finally been put to rest, so let us examine inflation from a purely scientific point of view.

Constructing a house using a standard, twelve-inch foot as your basic measure, is a straightforward task, providing you have the necessary skills as a carpenter. Suppose, however, that you have worked on a house for a week and have ordered a new supply of lumber. It is delivered, and you attempt to use it in your construction, but it is too short.

You call the supplier and complain about the "short" lumber, and he informs you that it is exactly what you ordered and exactly the length you specified. At first you are puzzled, but then you discover that the length of a foot has been altered. It is now ten inches instead of twelve inches. You are faced with a chaotic situation.

But this situation is exactly what we confront given our changing monetary standard, and it is why economic theory so often fails to explain economic relationships. If too much money chasing too few goods causes prices to rise, thus causing inflation, then there must be some sort of relationship between the quantity of money in the economy—the M1—and the total prices of all tangible assets and services, as well as the goods and services exchanged during one year.

Since the M1—cash and checkbook money in the hands of the nonbanking public—is designated in numbers and the price of all tangible assets and services are also designated in numbers, we can assume there is a mathematical relationship between the M1 and the total price of all tangible assets and services. We can also assume that this mathematical relationship is a direct one.

An economist once asserted, during a discussion on the various reasons for inflation, that if we doubled the money supply in the economy and leave the volume of all tangible assets and services unchanged, the price of these tangible assets and services would double.

On the other hand, if we halved the M1 and left the quantity of tangible assets and services unchanged, the prices of the tangible assets and services would also halve.

If we designate P as the aggregate price for all tangible assets and services, their volume remaining constant, then, according to this argument,

1. $2 \, M1 = 2 \times P$ or $2P$
2. $1/2 \, M1 = 1/2 \times P = 1/2P$
3. $M1 = P$

For equations one and two to be correct, equation three must be a truth; if equation three is not true, obviously neither will be equations one or two. Is equation three true? It is an undeniable fact that our standard of monetary measure is constantly changing—witness our preoccupation with inflation!

The M1 as of April 1990 was $785 billion, and the total price of all tangible assets and services was well into the tens of trillions of dollars. Therefore, equation three is not a truth, and thus equations one and two are also untrue. It follows that the statement "too much money chasing too few goods causes inflation" is blatantly false.

Traditional economists have too long been preoccupied with the so-called tautology MV = PQ in which M is the transaction money supply (M1), V is the velocity of money, P is the price of goods and services, and Q is the gross national product (GNP).

Results of such a formula can be predictable only if three of these four values are constants. This formula ignores the dynamic nature of the money supply (M1) that changes from hour to hour. Money is constantly being destroyed as loans are repaid. This formula totally ignores this factor and more importantly it ignores the all-debt nature of money and the millions of dollars that are being removed daily from the economic arena to pay interest to the money creators. Repayment of loans and interest reduce the M1—transaction money—that is the lifeblood of commerce and industry. In addition, velocity, prices, and GNP are continuously changing. *In fact, the formula, MV = PQ has no constant and scientifically is not only meaningless but is also useless.*

Until economists come to grips with the everchanging status of each of these values, economics will continue to enjoy the reputation of being an intellectually bankrupt discipline.

The Truth About Inflation

All the nations on earth, with two noteworthy exceptions named Guernsey and Jersey in the English Channel, have an all-debt money system. During the course of my research I contacted a professor of economics who correctly pointed out that in almost all foreign countries the monetary author-ity is the government—although there is a certain degree of independence bestowed on the central banks. The professor correctly claimed that the economic problems faced by all those countries are similar to the economic problems of the United States, where the monetary authority is in private hands.

I was perplexed by the economic problems faced by countries whose governments own their central banks. The reason, however, became clear after I interviewed an ex-banker from the Central Bank of El Salvador. When asked how the Central Bank of El Salvador creates money, he stated that the government prints interest-bearing bonds, turns them over to the Central Bank, then borrows money from its Central Bank. In addition, its commercial banks still use the fractional reserve deposit expansion banking system. So, although some countries own their central banks, all their money is created as debt. Although the money creation authority is different, the method of creating money is the same. In effect, then, they are not different.

Even countries that nationalized their banking industries and own their respective central banks use the all-debt money system. An all-debt money system means that all money is created as debt in a particular country, and the money is created by the banks. In the United States, all banks, includ-ing the twelve Federal Reserve banks, are privately owned, despite what one may read in a textbook on economics.

Even the courts have established that the Federal Reserve banks are privately owned.

Suppose all the money in existence in the economy totals $1 trillion. This sum has thus been borrowed from the banks, the money creators. As long as this money is in existence in the economy, it is a debt at interest owed to the banks and therefore must be repaid to them.

Let us assume that this trillion dollars was borrowed, regardless by whom, at a 10 percent annual interest, mainly to activate production of goods and services and to facilitate the transaction of goods and services. At the end of the year, the total debt to the banks will be $1 trillion of principal plus 10 percent or $100 billion dollars of interest. Can the aggregate debt be paid? Obviously the impossible mathematical demands of an all-debt money system are revealed, for the answer is a resounding "no." In such a scenario, those that are able to repay their aggregate debt have used someone else's borrowed principal to make their interest payments. Thus, those others will not be able to repay their total principal and interest. In an all-debt money system, for some to succeed, others must fail—they will fall victim to bankruptcies and business failures, even though they work hard and intelligently. The velocity of money has nothing to do with this impossible problem.

Let us now address the $100 billion of interest on the $1 trillion debt for the one-year period. The sum can either be removed from the M1 to pay the banks and thus decrease the M1 to $900 billion, or the borrowers can leave the $1 trillion dollars constant in the economy and borrow more money for their interest payments (the $100 billion). If the interest is borrowed, it will not enter the economy in the form of an increase in M1—the M1 does not increase to $1.1 trillion—but instead only generates more debt, the debt on the books of the bank will be increased to $1.1 trillion. And herein lies an important clue as to the real cause of inflation.

The third alternative is to combine the two scenarios, but no matter what course we take, one thing is certain—a $100 billion interest charge exists and is owed by the borrowers. If the $1 trillion was created all for commercial loans, *then the $100 billion of interest charged by the banks is a business expense to the borrowers and will be added to the cost of existing goods as such.* The costs are passed along to consumers in the form of price increases, and the unchanged quantities of goods and services now demand more dollars. To be more direct, the existing money supply has been devalued or debased because prices have gone up.

Because the existing money supply has been devalued by the interest payments, the purchasing power in the marketplace needs to be restored. This task can only be accomplished by further borrowing to pay interest and to continue the exchange of the higher priced goods and services. This further borrowing, which increases the money supply, is the reason conventional economists erroneously conclude that too much money causes inflation.

These economists have the cause and effect relationship reversed. Although it is true that during an inflationary period the money supply increases, one is not the cause of the other. This thinking on the part of economists is a monumental error in current economic theory.

The increased borrowing that increases the money supply during inflationary phases of the economy is necessary to meet interest charges and to facilitate the exchange of higher priced goods and services. These interest charges result from the unproductive interest charges that have become real business expenses.

If this borrowing did not occur to increase the M1, there would be a relative shortage in the M1 compared to the prices of goods and services and a recession or depression would be a certainty. Of course, there is the greed factor, or opportunism, dealt with earlier in this chapter. If retailers want to double their prices from one day to the next, there is no mechanism to stop them except normal competition. Government price controls can be effective in some cases, but, otherwise, greed or opportunism can be a secondary factor causing inflation.

Unquestionably, there are only three possible causes for the inflation phenomenon. These are the interest payments on commercial loans that devalue the existing money supply, greed or opportunism (the human foible that seeks something for nothing and devalues the existing money supply), and a law passed to devalue money.

Inflation, then, is best defined as: *A decrease in the purchasing power of money caused by demanding more debt money for the same goods and services. This demand mainly comes from increased business expenses resulting from interest payments on commercial loans. Greed and a lawful decree devaluing money are secondary factors that cause inflation.*

Chapter 7

Debt and Bondage

*Money is a new form of slavery, and distinguished from
the old simply by the fact that it is impersonal, that there is
no human relation between master and slave.*

Leo Tolstoy

"I see in the near future a crisis approaching that un-
nerves me and causes me to tremble for the safety of my
country; corporations have been enthroned, an era of corruption in high places will follow, and the money power of the
country will endeavor to prolong its reign by working upon
the prejudices of the people until the wealth is aggregated in
a few hands, and the Republic is destroyed."[1] Abraham
Lincoln spoke these words after the passage of the National
Banking Act in 1863. The ugly fact is that, through an
iniquitous monetary system, we have nationalized a system
of economic oppression that is equally as damnable as the
Lincoln era of chattel slavery. Our all-debt money system,
with its built-in debt generator called compound interest, has

resulted in irregular cycles of inflation, recession, and depression. These swings in the economy have contributed to immense human suffering due to bankruptcies, business failures, unemployment, and foreclosures.

Money has been a frequent topic of discussion throughout the ages. Some of the earliest references to money, and usury in particular, are found in the Bible. An example from *Ezekiel, Chapter 22, Verse 12* states, "In thee have they taken gifts to shed blood; thou hast taken usury and increase, and thou hast greedily gained of thy neighbors by extortion, and hast forgotten Me, saith the Lord God."

In the early years of our country, Thomas Jefferson, like Lincoln, was troubled by monetary developments in his era. He said,

> If the American people ever allow the banks to control the issuance of their currency, first by inflation, and then by deflation, the banks and corporations that will grow up around them will deprive the people of all property, until their children will wake up homeless on the continent their fathers occupied. The issuing power of money should be taken from the banks and restored to Congress and the people to whom it belongs. I sincerely believe the banking institutions having the issuing power of money, are more dangerous to liberty than standing armies.[2]

Lincoln observed, "The government should create, issue, and circulate all the currency and credit needed to satisfy the spending power of government and the buying power of consumers.[3] I might add that government should also create enough money to satisfy business needs. (Lincoln's foresight about corruption in high places has been fulfilled, and the corrupt government officials linked to the failures of some savings and loan institutions are now bearing testimony.) The privilege of creating and issuing money is not only the prerogative of government, but it is the government's greatest creative opportunity. By adopting these principles, the long-felt need for a uniform medium of exchange would be satisfied. The taxpayers would save immense sums of interest. The financing of all public enterprises and the conduct of the Treasury would become matters of practical administration. Money would cease to be the master and would become the servant of humanity.

Visionaries in the early years of our republic predicted problems with government debt. Georgia Congressman James Jackson, addressing the U.S. House of Representatives of the First Congress, predicted that debt would increase exponentially. Jackson opposed Alexander Hamilton's plan to use a funded debt to increase the money supply of the new nation when he said,

> Gentlemen may come forward perhaps, and tell me, that funding the public debt will increase the circulating medium of the country, by means of its transferable quality; but this is denied by the best informed men. The funding of the debt will occasion enormous taxes for the payment of interest. These taxes will bear heavily both on agriculture and commerce. It will be charging the active and industrious citizen . . . to pay the indolent and creditor. In the proportion that it benefits the one, it will depress the other.
>
> I contend that a (private) funding system in this country will be highly dangerous to the welfare of the Republic; it may, for a while, raise our credit and increase our circulation by multiplying a new species of currency; but it must hereafter settle upon our posterity a burden which they can neither bear nor relieve themselves from. It will establish a precedent in America that may, and in all

probability will, be pursued by the sovereign authority, until it brings upon us that ruin which it has never failed to bring (since the dawn of recorded history). Let us take warning by the errors of Europe, and guard against the introduction of a system followed by calamities so general. Though our present debt be but a few million, in the course of a single century it may be multiplied to an extent we dare not think of.[4]

Congressman Jackson's prophecy has been fulfilled. Our public debt is now well over $3 trillion and climbing exponentially. Obviously, Jackson had a clear and fundamental understanding of the inherent problems of a debt-dominant money system.

Whenever the private sector creates money out of thin air as debt and lends this money to the government, sooner or later such an act will lead to escalating government debt, high interest rates, high taxes, and political and economic instability.

Debt

"A national debt will be to us a national blessing."[5] These were the words of Alexander Hamilton, first secretary of the Treasury of the United States. Hamilton will be best remembered by some for his railroading of a charter through Congress in 1791 establishing the "First Bank of the United States."

One would erroneously assume, that since it was named the First Bank of the United States, the bank was chartered and owned by the government and operated by the national Treasury. Instead, the bank was privately owned and allowed to create paper—checkbook money—out of thin air, as well as to print private bank notes, and to lend them at interest to the U.S. government and to private businesses.

Some uninformed Americans consider Alexander Hamilton, the father of our public debt, an American hero. Although, Hamilton said that a national debt would be a blessing to the American taxpayer, in his heart he knew that such a debt would be a blessing for the private money creators, the bankers.

Public Debt

In a daily newspaper, on the television, or in a business magazine, you cannot escape the constant bombardment of accusations against the U.S. government about its spending habits. Everyone is concerned about public debt, but no one makes any rational or scientific proposal to solve it. Everyone blames excessive spending for our problems, when in reality government ought to be blamed for excessive borrowing.

Government is the natural target for the ventriloquists—economists, business reporters, assorted financial gurus, and out-and-out propagandist debt creators. Today our national debt is staggering, in a few tomorrows it will be mind-boggling.

Public debt is what the government owes to the privately owned Federal Reserve banks and other financial institutions, foreign governments and banks, and a few citizens both at home and abroad who hold government bonds. Current public debt is significantly in excess of $3 trillion.

Figure 4 reveals the staggering growth of the federal government's debt since 1836, when the debt was zero. From about 1836 until about 1914, public debt was negli-

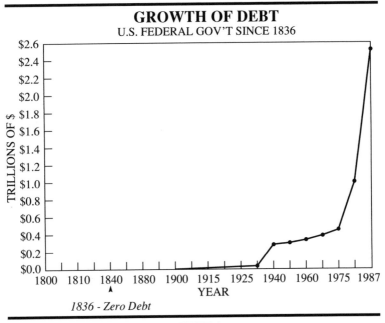

GROWTH OF DEBT
U.S. FEDERAL GOV'T SINCE 1836

FIGURE 4

gible. After 1914 and World War I, it began to climb, with a steep rise during World War II. Since about 1975 the growth in public debt has taken on epic proportions. Between 1975 and 1988 the debt rose from about $475 billion to more than $2.5 trillion. Current estimates place the public debt at much greater than $3 trillion. For most of us who cannot comprehend such large numbers, the percentage increase in debt in thirteen short years has been 426.32 percent, or more than 32 percent per year. How would you have handled this magnitude of increase in your own debt during the same thirteen-year period?

Assume that in 1975 you earned $50,000 annually and your salary increased at the rate of 5 percent per year. After thirteen years you are thus earning $94,282 annually. As-

Debt Virus

sume, also, that in 1975 you spent 90 percent of your earnings to liquidate your debt, saved 10 percent, and your debt increased at the same rate as that of the government's, or 32 percent yearly for the period. Today you are spending $361,748.62 annually, and your earnings are woefully inadequate to service your debt.

One should remember that public debt is debt that is owed by every American taxpayer. We are now not only overtaxing the working class American, we are also levying taxes on our children, who are not yet working. If the public debt was $2.5 trillion at the end of 1987 and the population of the United States at the end of 1987 was 250 million, then every living American was in debt to the tune of $10,000—even newborn Americans.

Figure 5, constructed from basic data provided by the Department of the Treasury, Office of Management and

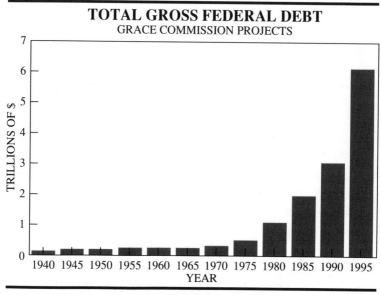

FIGURE 5

Budget for fiscal year 1986, shows that our projected national debt will be over $6 trillion by 1995. Even if the population of the United States in 1995 grows to 300 million, each newborn will be heir to a $20,000 national debt . . . and the figure rises exponentially. Our children are thus being born indentured to a debt-dominant money system, owned and controlled by a handful of private citizens, solely for their personal gain.

Interest on Federal Debt

In 1836 our federal debt was zero and our interest charge was zero. In 1991, if one assumes that government is paying an interest rate of 10 percent on its debt and its total debt is $3 trillion, its annual interest charge is $300 billion. If the government spends $1 trillion in 1991, then 30 percent of the total government expenditures will go to service interest obligations. If there is a deficit in the government's budget for 1991, the government will borrow more money and the $3 trillion debt will increase even more.

As we can see from Table 4, a debt of $1,000 in circulation at 10 percent compound interest generates an annual interest charge that is greater than all the money in circulation. Somewhere between the fifth and tenth year, the annual *interest* payment becomes greater than the circulating principal or the M1—cash and checkbook money in the hands of the nonbanking public.

Examine Figure 6. The interest on the federal debt has been growing at an exponential rate. It is possible to project the interest growth into the future to determine the magnitude of the annual interest on the national debt, based on what has occurred in the past.

GROWTH OF INT. DEBT VS. MONEY SUPPLY, M1

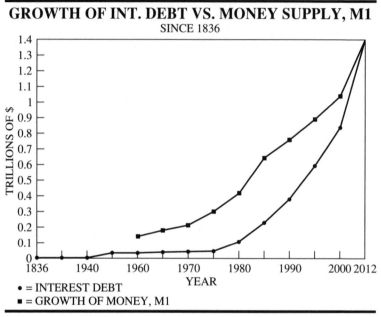

• = INTEREST DEBT
■ = GROWTH OF MONEY, M1

FIGURE 6

TABLE 5
GROWTH OF M1, 1960–1985

Year	M1 (Billions of $)
1960	141.8
1965	169.5
1970	216.6
1975	291.1
1980	414.2
1985	626.6
1987 (Jan.)	744.4

"Economic Report of the President," January 1987
"Federal Reserve Bulletin," April, 1987.

The growth in the M1 is detailed in the "Economic Report of the President" sent to Congress in January of 1987.[6] Table 5 shows the growth of the M1 between 1960 and 1987.

If you plot the values of the M1 presented in Table 5 onto Figure 6 and project these curves into the future, it becomes apparent that the growth of interest on the federal debt and the growth of the M1 intersect at about the year 2012, based on historical growth rates.

If we assume that the present public debt grows at the same exponential rate as in the past and that the M1, the volume of money available for immediate spending in the economy, also grows at its same exponential rate, the annual interest on the total public debt will be equal to or greater than the M1, that is, all the money in circulation, by about the year 2012 (see Figure 6). At this time, the bubble will burst, and there will occur a total financial collapse in the United States. Major stockholders in the Federal Reserve banks will benefit from this collapse, but not many others.

A word of caution. This purely mathematical approach does not take into account the interest payments being continually removed from the M1 by the private sector on debts in the private sector. This money is removed to pay private banks. With this point in mind, the reduction of available money in the economy could lead to a financial collapse earlier than shown in the graph.

Private Debt

Table 6 shows that between 1977 and 1986, Exxon Corporation paid $5.83 billion in interest for its borrowings. Interest payments are a business expense and get passed along as part of the price of goods and services. Consumers

TABLE 6
EXXON CORP. – INTEREST EXPENSES

Year	Interest Expense (millions of $)
1977	399
1978	425
1979	494
1980	669
1981	780
1982	670
1983	749
1984	400
1985	627
1986	<u>614</u>
TOTAL	5827 (million $)

"Exxon Corp., 1986 Financial and Statistical Supplement to the Annual Report," pages 4 & 5.

of the products of Exxon Corporation actually pay for the interest expense of Exxon.

As consumers, then, we not only pay the interest payment on money we individually borrow from money creators, but we also pay the interest payments on the debts of thousands of corporations and businesses whose products and services we utilize. And total debt has also been growing exponentially since 1960—see Table 7. This is a fine system for the money creators, but isn't it time we call a halt to this added cost of doing business where no value is added to the product?

Freedom

The preamble to the *U.S. Constitution* states, "We the people of the United States, in order to form a more perfect

TABLE 7
GROWTH OF TOTAL (PRIVATE & PUBLIC)
DEBT: IN U.S.

Year	Debt (billions of $)
1960	708.2
1965	990.8
1970	1410.6
1975	2245.6
1980	3898.8
1985	6778.6
1986 (Dec.)	7597.2

"Economic Report of the President to Congress," January, 1987
"Federal Reserve Bulletin," April, 1987

TOTAL DEBT OF U.S.
PUBLIC AND PRIVATE

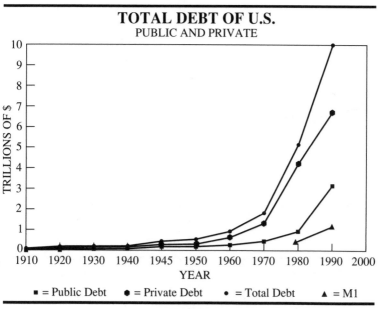

■ = Public Debt ● = Private Debt • = Total Debt ▲ = M1

FIGURE 7

Union, establish justice, ensure domestic tranquility, provide for the common defense, promote the general welfare, and secure the blessings of liberty to ourselves and our posterity, do ordain and establish this constitution for the United States of America."

Do we have the true liberty and freedom guaranteed in the words of this document? Most people are busy searching for the American dream, forgetting that *dreams are only for those who are asleep.*

It is time to wake up. All freedom is dependent upon economic freedom, which is having the ability to produce goods and services without monetary constraints, that leads to price stability, efficiency, growth, and equity. We do not have economic freedom in this country because of a fundamental flaw in our monetary system, and without it, who can dare say we are free?

Free Enterprise

Economists and bankers, as well as media propagandists for the special interest groups and self-serving "experts," are busy spreading the myth that we have a free enterprise system in the United States. How can we have a free enterprise system when the ingredient necessary to make the economy function, namely money, is under the control of a few citizens in the private sector? If I created and controlled the money supply of a nation, it wouldn't make any difference to me who made the laws. The opportunity to create money is the most awesome power one can have over mankind and civilization.

During a conversation between President Andrew Jackson and Nicholas Biddle, president of the privately owned First Bank of the United States, Biddle supposedly said,

"Andy, if I want, I can destroy any segment of the economy in this country."

"How is that Nick?" Old Hickory questioned.

"Simply by restricting credit," Biddle replied.

"Then by God, I will destroy your bank," Jackson bristled.[7] And he did, but only for a while; the private bank charters were later granted to a handful of private citizens who continued to create and control the money of the nation.

The money creators, by withholding credit, can cause an economic depression at will. For all the speculations as to the cause of the recession of 1920-1921, document No. 310 of the U.S. Senate for the sixty-seventh Congress, fourth session, provides a clear answer to what happened. If one reads the minutes of that meeting, it can quickly be discerned that it was the gradual contraction of the money supply that eventually led to this recession.

The contraction of money volume—M1—is a mechanism that dispossesses the productive elements of society and transfers their wealth into the hands of the money creators through bankruptcies, foreclosures, and unemployment. The Great Depression of 1929 was similarly engineered.

When all wealth is transferred into a few hands through business failures and seizures, production will cease. When you take all a man produces, he refuses to work. He will seek another means to make a living. Crime is the most obvious avenue. In the past, when human beings have been pushed to the limit and have been dispossessed of all their belongings, pogroms have always resulted.

Chapter 8

Money and Banks

Banking was conceived in iniquity and born in sin. Bankers own the earth. Take it away from them, but leave them the power to create money, and with the flick of a pen, they will create enough money to buy it back again and again.
Josiah Stamp, Former President, Bank of England.

The Story of Money

The story of money is actually comprised of two parts. The first explains how our ancestors developed a "medium of exchange" to enable them to buy goods and services, measure their worth, and save for the future. The second is a saga of our evolution from a society of self-sufficient beings, who made what they needed and swapped their goods for items they wanted, to a society in which money plays the most important role.

Any item, tobacco, shark's teeth, iron nails, or fish hooks, can be used as money if it is generally accepted in payment for goods, services, debts, and taxes. In the United States we use coin, paper currency, and checkbook money. Most of us get money by working, and we use these wages to purchase goods and services.

A standard currency allows us to compare the value of different items with a single standard or unit of measurement, a yardstick of value. We can compare the cost of an automobile and a motorcycle and measure their worth in terms of the hours we must work to earn enough money to buy each one.

Our purchases provide those who produce the goods with money to pay their workers and other expenses. Workers and producers use part of the monies they earn from their labors to pay federal, state, and local taxes. Governments use these taxes to build roads and hospitals and to pay soldiers, teachers, and the myriad of other government workers. Tax money is thus collected and then spent back into the economy by government workers who earn wages from the government.

Many of us save money, often depositing it in financial institutions such as banks and credit unions or in pension plans. Banks use this money as a base to create new checkbook money, which they lend to workers, producers, and governments requiring additional funds. As long as the money flowing into financial institutions matches the outflow, the total amount of money in circulation remains unchanged.

The commercial bank creates the bulk of new money—checkbook money—when it makes loans and investments. Producers and workers borrowing from commercial banks spend this "new" money into circulation when they make purchases. Thrifts also create money when they lend. The ability of banks to expand the amount of money circulating allows our economy to grow.

If money is working well, it should purchase the same amount of goods and services from year to year. If this were so, then money would serve as an excellent store of value. Since the consumer price index has been rising steadily since 1900, however, money obviously has not been holding its purchasing power very well.

Ponder this cycle carefully for a moment. The principal of a loan is created and spent into circulation, but the interest charged on that principal is never created. The nature of the loan requires that interest be paid on the loan. The interest must come from "within the system" since it is not created. It is, therefore, impossible to repay the total debt, principal, and interest.

In simplest terms, the uncreated interest accumulates as debt, which is passed on in the price of goods. This rise in the price of existing goods is a demand for more debt-dollars for the same goods, thus money loses its purchasing power.

How It All Began

Man developed money because of a basic instinct, the desire to acquire something he did not have, could not find, and could not produce himself. When our ancestors first satisfied their wants by exchanging their goods, bartering began.

Archaeologists believe that European and Asian tribes routinely met to exchange goods in the Ural Mountains about twelve-thousand years ago. The barter system worked well for thousands of years, but it was troublesome. "Wants" had to match exactly. A farmer offering corn for a mule had to find a mule owner who wanted corn. If the mule swapper wanted an ax instead of corn, then the farmer was out of luck. He could search for an ax maker who would take corn and then traded for the mule, but searching took time and was inconvenient. It was not always possible to find a match so that a trade could be made.

Because bartering required a "double coincidence" of matching wants, people could not buy many things through exchange alone. Prices were also a problem. On a given day, four axes might be exchanged for a mule or small cow but not for a bushel of corn. Weeks later, a hungry toolmaker might swap many axes for a bushel of corn, and so it went. It became increasingly difficult to agree on a "standard of value" for making the exchanges.

With the barter system, it was difficult to save, that is, to store up purchasing power. Apples might be valuable in the fall, but if held too long, no one would want them. With the development of permanent communities and a more organized society, bartering on a large scale became totally unworkable. Although bartering has largely disappeared, it is still used in some instances today, especially between nations.

Commodity Money

As time passed, nations saw that solving the problems inherent in the barter system required adoption of a standard "medium of exchange." At first, common items were used. Commodities like salt and cattle were often used. These items were generally accepted because their usefulness made them valuable in and of themselves. But many of the commodities had built-in drawbacks, limiting their usefulness as money.

A good money must be easy to handle, serve as a standard of value, and possess a uniform measurement of relative worth. It should be easy to divide into fractional parts, and one should be able to accumulate it to use at a later date—to "save" it. Should it be scarce? Absolutely not!

Despite the obvious drawbacks, commodity forms of money were used for thousands of years. In the 1700s, grain, fish, gunpowder, and shot were some of the popular forms of American commodity money. The Yap Islanders in the Pacific used massive stone "money" wheels until World War II. Masai warriors of Africa, even today, use cattle money to purchase brides.

Precious Metal Money

It is not known precisely where precious metals were first used as money. Widely separated societies at different times in history became attracted to the glitter and beauty of silver and gold, which were used to make jewelry and sacred objects. Zinc and lead were also used as money.

Mercantilism

In the seventh century, European countries followed an economic system known as "mercantilism." The mercantilists believed that nations remained powerful and wealthy by amassing gold and silver. They established colonies and took raw materials and precious metals from the new lands they conquered while selling goods to the peoples of these lands.

In 1776, the Scottish philosophy professor Adam Smith published a landmark book, *The Wealth of Nations*. In this tome, Smith argued that the source of national power and wealth was not gold and silver but the production of goods. Smith's book became the cornerstone of the new social science called "economics." His writings and those of his contemporaries slowly turned Europe toward improving production and developing interdependent trade. But Adam Smith lacked a precise knowledge of the science of money. What Smith did not know, he could not teach his subsequent followers, the present-day economists. Nevertheless, his work marked the beginning of the social science of economics.

Gold and Silver

Many people sought gold and silver because the metals were scarce and hard to find. Precious metals could command more goods than most other commodities. The Chinese used gold cubes as early as 2100 B.C.

The Bible mentions precious metals. Solomon demonetized silver during his reign, thus reducing the volume of money in circulation. This action brought about distress and a rebellion led by Jeroboam. Silver was used even before the time of Solomon, however. Abraham used silver to pay for the cave of Machpelah, used as a sepulcher for Sarah. It is also written in the Bible that Judas Iscariot "betrayed Jesus for 30 pieces of silver."

Coins

The Lydians in west Turkey cast the earliest known coins around 700 B.C. These were crudely inscribed gold and silver pellets. But gold and silver coins were not immune to problems. Alexander the Great brought so much precious metal home from his conquests that the value of gold and silver in Macedonia was reduced by one-third because of the shortage of goods and services.

Paper Money

A new form of money emerged in Europe because large quantities of coin were bulky and unsafe to carry. People going on long trips began to leave their coins with gold-smiths for safekeeping. They received receipts for the gold they left behind, and at their destination the receipts were exchanged for coins. These receipts became so popular that people began paying debts with them rather than drawing their coins out of the "goldsmith depository." This step marked the beginning of paper currency.

Checks

Around the same time, people began paying bills with letters instructing goldsmiths to pay the holders of the letters with gold coins. These letters marked the beginning of an-other phase in our saga of money. These letters were the first "checks."

Paper Money in America

Paper money, which the Chinese were already using around A.D.1200, grew fastest in coin-poor America. Com-modity money was being substituted fairly well for scarce coin among the colonists, but it was not sufficient for their government. In the late 1600s, several colonies issued paper money to pay bills until enough taxes could be collected in gold and silver to buy the paper back. As long as the colonists believed the paper would be bought back or redeemed, it was accepted. If there were any doubts, though, the paper was not accepted.

The other paper money problems were well known. The Continental Congress, needing to finance an army but lacking taxing power, turned to the printing press. Congress issued so much nonproductive paper money it resulted in "inflation"—a condition of soaring prices that made people bitterly opposed to the government issuance of paper money. Without taxing power, the Continental Congress could not extinguish the "paper money" it had spent into circulation, an action erroneously believed necessary to prevent "inflation." Vendors of goods and services falsely believed that too much money made money less "valuable," so they demanded more of such money for the same goods and services.

"The 'Continental,' as the government-issued paper money was called, became worthless, not only because there were shortages of commodities, but also because it was easy to counterfeit, and the English did exactly that."[1]

Thus was born the saying, "Not worth a Continental."

Early paper monies were promissory notes (IOUs) that represented claims on precious metals. They could be redeemed at a goldsmith or treasury. In 1968, backing paper money, namely Federal Reserve notes, by precious metals was abolished in the United States of America.

Banks and Thrifts

Most of us view banks and thrifts as financial supermarkets servicing our individual financial needs. But they play a more important role in our economy by acting as financial intermediaries. As go-betweens, they link savers and borrowers and, at the same time, perform a variety of services for people and businesses paying and receiving money.

You can go into a bank with a bucket full of coins and exchange the coins for currency. You go to a bank for loans or to exchange leftover francs for dollars. You can get a home improvement loan, or you can use a bank as an overnight safety deposit box.

Types of Banks

In the United States today there are two major types of banking organizations: commercial banks and thrift institutions. "Thrifts" include savings and loan associations, savings banks, and credit unions. Generally, thrifts concentrate on providing a place for savings accounts and for making home loans to finance home mortgages.

"When banks and thrifts lend, they create new checkbook money by adding funds to borrowers' checking accounts. Since commercial banks create nearly three-quarters of new checkbook money, they have a special role in our financial system."[2]

People want their cash safe and well-protected. They deposit their money in thrifts, which have vaults, alarms, and deposit insurance. There is no doubt that your money is safer in a bank vault than in the mattress or a cookie jar at home.

Types of Accounts

You select an account based on how you intend to use the account. If you are saving for a new car, a vacation trip, or for Christmas, you put your money in a savings account.

However, if you plan to spend the money in the near future and want it available when you need it, you place your money in a checking account so that you can issue checks on the account.

There are various types of checking accounts. Deposits in checking accounts make up the bulk of the U.S. money supply—the M1. The rest is in currency and coin. By simply writing a check, you tell the bank to transfer money from your checking account to someone else's possession, either in an account or in the banking and goldsmith's form of cash. A check is not money, but rather an order to transfer money from an account.

History of Banking

Banking began thousands of years ago. The Assyrians, Babylonians, and ancient Greeks all practiced primitive forms of banking primarily in connection with trade—holding coins for safekeeping, exchanging foreign coins, and making loans. Ancient Rome had two types of bankers, those who made loans and those who exchanged foreign money for Roman money.

Banking grew rapidly in the Middle Ages when trade began to flourish. One of the oldest banking systems was in Italy. Banks were established in Venice in 1171 and in Genoa in 1320.

British banking began almost by accident in the mid-1600s when King Charles I helped himself to the money that merchants had left in his protection in the Tower of London. Although the king later returned the money he had taken, merchants could not trust him and had their clerks protect their funds instead. But the clerks often stole or secretly borrowed the merchants' money and lent it to goldsmiths.

These goldsmiths borrowed the money from the clerks at an interest rate lower than the interest rate at which they subsequently lent it. Borrowing and lending in this manner was so profitable that the goldsmiths expanded their operations by soliciting money from the public. *Business grew because they promised safekeeping and an interest payment on the deposits under their care.*

Goldsmiths gave depositors receipts for their funds. These receipts, which could be used as money, marked the beginning of modern-day checks. *Since the receipts were accepted as money, the goldsmiths soon made loans with receipts instead of gold.* They were "creating money," a move that changed them from goldsmiths into bankers.

American Banking

American banking as we know it today started in America when the Bank of North America was formed in Philadelphia in 1781 to help finance the American Revolution.

In colonial times, banks issued notes, IOUs, when they made loans. These loans were generally backed by land. As time passed, other banks sprang up around the country. The Bank of New York, one of the first American banks, opened in 1784 with a charter drawn up by Alexander Hamilton, who believed that America's future laid in industrialization and that the country needed a strong banking system to help build industries.

Hamilton proposed that Congress charter a bank patterned after the Bank of England, which was a private bank. History will ultimately acknowledge this move as a monumental mistake in American financial history. Congress approved the idea and chartered the First Bank of the United States in 1791, despite strong opposition from those who feared centralized power over money. The bank was chartered for a period of twenty years, and at the end of this period, the charter was not renewed. However, a Second Bank of the United States was chartered in 1816. That bank also lasted for twenty years, and the charter was not renewed.

Like all banks of that era, the two banks of the United States issued their own paper currency and exchanged currency for silver or gold. When customers deposited notes issued by state-chartered banks, these notes were quickly returned to the issuing bank and redeemed for precious metal.

Easterners were pleased with this redemption policy because they erroneously believed it helped limit the amount of paper currency in circulation and thereby restrained inflation. Westerners in the frontier states like Kentucky and Tennessee felt that state bank notes were redeemed too quickly, leaving too little money for their expanding economy.

President Andrew Jackson forced the closing of the Second Bank of the United States in 1836. The number of state banks and the amount of notes they issued expanded steadily afterwards. These banks played an important role in America's rapid growth. State bank loans helped finance the purchase of farm land, seeds, tools, and livestock. They also helped build factories producing such new tools as the cotton gin, steel plow, and reaper. Banks also helped finance the railroads and steamboats that transported farm products to the cities and manufactured goods to the farms.

Early Monetary Problems

When the Civil War began, America didn't have a uniform national currency. Several thousand different notes were in circulation. They were of different sizes, colors, and designs. The value of these notes depended on how much trust people had in the issuing bank. Trust was also a problem for banks. They wanted to be sure their notes were accepted at face value and that any notes they accepted from other banks were worth face value.

Around this time, the government was having trouble getting investors, mainly banks, to buy bonds being sold to finance the Civil War. In 1863, the Treasury solved both problems by creating federally chartered national banks that were allowed to issue their own notes based on the amount of federal bonds they held. The notes would all look alike, except for the name of the issuing bank. Since they were backed by government bonds, people would have faith in the currency.

State banks were at first indifferent to the idea, but some signed up as national banks when Congress increasingly taxed state notes. Although the tax diminished the number of these notes in circulation, many state banks flourished since the use of checks was reducing the importance of bank notes. The state banks did not have to issue notes to lend but could simply create checkbook money that was acceptable as money.

Under this dual system of both state and federally chartered banks, the number of state banks climbed very rapidly from a handful of banks in 1870 to about twenty thousand in 1913.

National banks helped strengthen the banking system and create a national currency, but there were still many weaknesses. One problem was that smaller banks around the country sent their reserves to major banks, where they were "lent" to businesses. Sometimes when the smaller banks tried to get their reserves back to use in their own areas, they found that the bigger banks had used their deposits as a base for creating more checkbook money. There would thus be a delay in the return of cash to the smaller banks. Occasionally some of the smaller banks ran out of cash and had to close their doors. One bank closing sometimes led depositors in other banks to demand their cash, forcing yet more closings. The worst of these economy-shaking "bank panics" occurred in 1907.

Chapter 9

Banking and the Goldsmiths

So, I'll enjoy my 10 percent and bless those mighty men who first invented the compound interest on the indebtedness of governments and men.

To prevent future financial panics and bank failures like that of 1907, Congress established the Federal Reserve System in 1913 after long study and much debate. Although the idea was to prevent a recurrence of the financial panic of 1907, history has proven that this action only served to sap the productive elements of American society of a significant portion of the fruits of their labors.

The Federal Reserve System was supposed to avoid financial panics, recessions, and economic depressions and to stabilize the purchasing power of our currency. Yet, we suffered the most devastating depression in our history in 1929, a mere sixteen years later. *Additionally, a 1990 dollar is now worth no more than six cents when compared with the 1900 dollar* (see Table 3).

Where is the stability in the purchasing power of the currency, and for whose benefit was the Federal Reserve System set up? These questions beg for clear, definitive answers.

Many in this country are worried about another economic depression, a depression that will make 1929 look like a Sunday afternoon picnic. This impending depression is supposed to occur within the next decade. Can it happen?

There is no way it cannot, and the timing is totally at the discretion of the private banks—the Federal Reserve System. If the money creators decide to have a depression, they can start the inevitable slide into it by withholding credit. But even if they do not withhold credit, another devastating economic depression is looming in the near future because such an event is part and parcel of a debt-dominant monetary system where interest charges increase the debt exponentially.

Ancient Goldsmith Banking

Our present monetary system is the result of a long, evolutionary process. Its mechanics began with the ancestors of our present bankers, the goldsmith bankers. They are the forebearers of the basic principles underlying our modern monetary machine.

The goldsmith bankers were private bankers who did practically all the banking business in Western Europe during the seventeenth century and before. People who possessed gold deposited it with the goldsmiths for safekeeping. The goldsmith then gave the customer a "claim check" or a receipt for his gold. Anyone having such a receipt in his possession could go to the goldsmith and reclaim the gold on deposit.

In time, these receipts became transferable and began circulating as money. People learned they could carry on trade and commerce by passing the goldsmith's receipts from hand to hand without ever drawing their gold from the vaults of the goldsmith. The goldsmiths were thus led to a system that has been a primary principle of banking ever since; namely, "fractional reserve deposit expansion."

Fractional Reserve Deposit Expansion

When the goldsmiths realized that few people were both-ering to claim their gold, they saw that they- could make loans with the gold that had been left in their safekeeping. That is, they could write out receipts for gold to borrowers who were actually borrowing ownership of the gold already in possession of the goldsmith. This gold, or, more accu-rately, the certificate of ownership of the gold was not the goldsmith's to lend; but as long as the calls for gold by the original depositors were infrequent, the goldsmith felt he could lend without undue risk and earn interest on a certain portion of the deposited gold. In other words, the goldsmith wrote receipts to people who were not depositing gold. These receipts were circulated as money, consequently receipts for more gold than the goldsmith actually had in his vault were in circulation. The specie was not debt, but the receipts evolved into interest-bearing debt.

The goldsmith had only a fraction of the gold needed to meet the claims against him should all receipts be redeemed for gold at the same time; thus the name "fractional reserve system." In the same way, when the banks in the United States kept their reserves in gold, the reserves amounted to only a small fraction of the amount of the money they issued, all of which was guaranteed to be redeemable in gold. We all know the currencies we use in the United States today are not backed by gold and have not been since 1968. In reality our currency is backed by nothing more than the government's ability to tax its citizens, and checkbook money has never, at any time in our history, been backed by gold.

"Runs" on Banks

The *Texas Bank Directors Handbook* of 1984 states,"The essence of banking in the United States is attracting deposits from the general public as a source of funds and then lending out those funds in the form of commercial loans."[1] That statement does not stand the test of logic, however. The money someone deposits in a bank for safekeeping becomes a liability of the bank, something the bank owes to the individual who made the deposit. Banks cannot lend their liabilities any more than you or I can.

"It is very difficult to remove from the minds of many people the impression that banks lend the money deposited with them," was the testimony of the secretary of the New Zealand Treasury in 1955 before a Royal Commission on Banking.[2] He and others admitted that banks do not lend their deposits. They explained that deposits are liabilities, and a bank cannot lend its liabilities. What, then, do they lend? They lend funds that the fractional reserve deposit system creates—checkbook money made with the stroke of a pen.

Further evidence of this truth was produced in 1939. "The banks cannot, of course, loan the money of their savings depositors," Graham Towers, governor of the Bank of Canada, told the Canadian government's Committee on Banking and Commerce. Mr. Towers continued, "They (commercial banks), by their activities in making loans and investments, create liabilities for themselves, and call these liabilities 'deposits.' "[3]

If commercial banks do lend out only savings deposit funds, how does growth in the M1 occur? If the depositors' money is lent out, as some claim, there cannot be any growth in the M1 since transferring a saver's funds from one person's account to another person's account adds no new money. But, each time a bank makes a loan, it is creating new money, a point that was well established earlier in this text.

Under the goldsmith system, the money supply could balloon, but this balloon could also quickly deflate. After all, the goldsmith banker was "playing the odds" at all times. He was gambling that the gold on deposit with him, or even a high proportion of his receipts, would not all at once be "called," that is, presented for return.

If this did happen, he would not be able to honor the claims against him, for he could not make quick collections from the people to whom he had lent money. Obviously the whole system would collapse. His money—the gold receipts he issued—would become worthless. Individual savings, the deposits of gold he had, would be wiped out. Many business enterprises would be forced into bankruptcy when gold receipts became void of purchasing power. The economic life of a community would be paralyzed for a time.

Since most people who accepted the goldsmith's money believed the goldsmith had enough gold to pay off his receipts in total, there was no need for holders of receipts to demand gold in payment. The more suspicious, those who doubted there was enough gold to honor the receipts outstanding, were dangerous since they could cause a run on the goldsmith and collapse the system.

"At one time, a banker of Amsterdam, an important center of European goldsmith banking, proposed a law making it a hanging offense to start a 'run' on a goldsmith. This immediately produced just such a 'run.' Of course, the gold-smith could not pay, and the customers ended up hanging the goldsmith."[4]

This kind of disaster was not the only shortcoming of the goldsmith system. A serious problem was posed by gold-smith money—the goldsmith receipts. They were usually acceptable only in the locality where the goldsmith was known. Businessmen and traders who wanted to make large transactions in foreign commerce or between different geographical regions often made huge withdrawals of gold for this exchange. This withdrawal, too, could bring about a collapse.

Like the powerful bankers who succeeded them, some of the bigger goldsmith bankers were not free from suspicion that they deliberately precipitated economic depressions at times. When business firms were forced into bankruptcy, valuable assets could be bought up at bargain prices by those who possessed sufficient money or could create it for themselves.

Usury Versus Interest

Usury may be the oldest "racket" practiced by the an-cient temple priests and nobles. The word "usury" appears in the second book of the Bible in Exodus, written by Moses fifteen hundred years before the birth of Christ. The writers of the *Old Oxford English Dictionary* explain its meaning: "The root word for usury is 'us-sus,' past participle of 'uti,' which means to use or exploit."[5]

The *Jewish Encyclopedia*, Volume II, tells us, "The Bib-lical law in all dealings among the Israelites forbids all 'increase' of debt by reason of lapse of time or forbearance, be the rate of interest high or low."[6] This statement brings out the important point that "interest," whether high or low, is not the only problem in the practice of usury. It is "time" and "debt at interest" that are the parasitic factors that gravitate the "increase" into the possession of the usurers.

When usurious interest rates are low, the gravitation of debtors' collateral assets to the usurer is slow. However, in our recent past (1979-1983), when the usurious prime and other interest rates were as high as 20 percent, the pledged collateral assets of individuals, businesses, industry, farmers, and others flowed into the possession of the usurers like rivers in the Rockies in springtime due to business failures and bankruptcies. The *U.S. Statistical Abstract* shows that during the period of high prime interest rates, industrial and commercial business failures jumped from about 7,500 in 1979 to about 12,000 in 1980, to about 17,000 in 1981, and to about 25,000 in 1982.[7]

Some sources imply that the difference between usury and interest is only a matter of degree; that is, if the interest rate is low it is considered "interest" and if the interest is high, or above some arbitrary legal limit, the interest is called "usury." Facts and logic point to a different conclusion, however.

The correct definition of common interest should read as follows: Any interest, high or low, charged on "personal" monies or funds loaned to anyone, for any purpose, is not usury, for the person is lending something that he actually possesses. Any interest, high or low, earned from a loan or deposit of personal money in a savings type institution is likewise not usury. Such interest paid and earned is not usurious because it does not add to or remove any money from the aggregate circulating M1 money supply.

On the other hand, "usury" is any interest charge, either high or low, charged by a lender who creates the lending funds either electronically or by bookkeeping entry. Such funds add to the circulating money supply—the M1. The interest charge thus paid to the money lender removes a percentage of the previously increased M1 money supply, rendering the total loaned principal mathematically unpayable.

In banking terms, there are two types of interest rates, the prime and the discount rate. A common myth circulating in the financial and economic world states that the prime rate charged by banks is dependent on the discount rate set by the Federal Reserve banks. Is there any truth to this statement? "Depository institutions sometimes borrow from the Federal Reserve to cover temporary, and often unexpected, deposit drains. The rate of interest that the Federal Reserve charges on these short-term loans is known as a discount rate. The discount rate has little direct effect on market interest rates such as the prime rate," according to a publication of the Federal Reserve Bank of Boston.[8]

There is another widely held misconception that banks borrow money from the Federal Reserve at the discount rate and then lend the funds at a higher rate to make a profit.

Fed loans are not designed to meet a continuing need for funds. Periodically, banks can suffer reserve deficiencies when depositors unexpectedly make large withdrawals or when loan demand rises beyond anticipated levels. A bank faced with a temporary reserve deficiency has various options. The bank can adjust its assets and liabilities by turning down new loan requests; by obtaining new deposits; by selling off some investments, such as government securities; or by borrowing in the money market. Or it can borrow at the Federal Reserve bank (discount window) for a relatively short period. Federal Reserve bank officers keep a careful record of how much banks are borrowing, how often, and for how long. A bank that relies too heavily on the discount window can expect a call from one of the Fed's officers to discuss the reasons for his borrowings. Borrowings at the discount window by large banks with access to national money markets are typically for only one day at a time. These larger banks are expected to try to satisfy their short term liquidity needs by borrowing the reserves elsewhere before approaching the Federal Reserve.[9]

Many people mistakenly believe that the Federal Reserve has direct control over the prime rate. Rather, the prime is determined by individual banks; that is, it is an administered rate. Banks do not earn money by borrowing money from the Federal Reserve banks at a lower interest rate and then lending those funds out at a higher interest rate. Neither do they lend out depositors' money, as they so insistently claim. *Instead, they create the money they lend or invest out of thin air, either electronically on a computer or with a pen on the ledgers of the bank as a bookkeeping entry.* In other words, they are lending or investing money that really doesn't exist. By what authority do they do this? I have asked a number of attorneys who are familiar with banking laws, and none could give me an answer. Wouldn't you, the reader, like to be able to lend something you do not have and charge a fee for doing so?

Bank Failures

Every economist and so-called business expert is familiar with the bell curve in Exhibit 12. This curve illustrates the different stages of a business cycle. There is a peak, followed by a contraction, followed by a trough, followed by an expansionary phase. This expansion then reaches a peak and the cycle starts all over again. Many believe that such cycles correspond to the universal cycles of nature and must go on ad infinitum. Such beliefs are blatantly false.

EXHIBIT 12
BUSINESS CYCLE STAGES

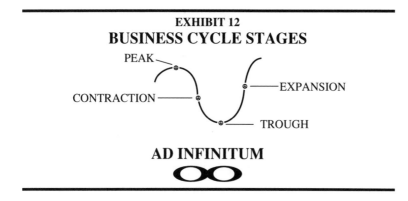

AD INFINITUM

The cycles of inflation, recession, and depression, unlike the regular cycles of nature, are totally irregular and lack predictability. These cycles are related more to the shortage of debt-free money in our debt-dominant money system. Irregularities in business cycles are due to variables in interest rates and the number of borrowers in the economic arena.

The "Doom" experiment shows that in an all-debt or debt-dominant money system, inflation is caused by a continuous withdrawal of money from the M1 to pay nonproductive interest to the money creators. The increase in M1 during the expansion phase is due to increased borrowing by the public—not only to start up new businesses in this so-called boom phase but also to pay increasing interest on debts and to maintain a sufficient amount of money in circulation to facilitate the exchange of existing goods and services.

In the past, this inflationary spiral or expansionary phase in the economic cycle has been erroneously attributed to too much money chasing too few goods. This thinking has been held by commercial banks, Federal Reserve banks, and some prominent economists since the publication of *The Wealth of Nations* by Adam Smith in 1776. To prevent this inflation, which is really caused by nonproductive interest payments that reduce the M1, banks further decrease the money supply by withholding credit, making it difficult for the public to borrow. This reduction in the size of the money supply causes a shortage of money in the hands of consumers, who do not have sufficient funds to buy goods and services.

Thus, *an economic contraction in demand occurs,* and the recessionary cycle begins. During this phase, unemployment rises and bankruptcies and foreclosures occur. The banks must write off some of their debts and take losses; some may even fail. To reverse this trend so they can again make profits, banks ease up the restraints on credit and encourage borrowing to activate the production of goods and services. We leave the trough, go back to the expansion phase, and begin the whole cycle over again.

Such cycles of inflation, recession, and depression are symptomatic of an all-debt or debt-dominant money system in which the cause of inflation is totally misunderstood by the so-called experts. It is the elasticity in the money supply created by mounting debt that causes the rise and fall of economic fortunes. As debt mounts, an ever-increasing portion of the money supply is retired to meet interest payments, and the economy is deprived of the money it needs to activate the production and transfer of goods and services.

When one asks a banker, an economist, or a bank advisor the reason for bank failures, the reasons invariably given are that loans were bad, banks were mismanaged, or times were hard. Let us examine each of these reasons.

Consider bad loans. Are we suggesting here that the lending officers know loans are bad when they made them? If so, such officers should not be working in banks. More importantly, they should be made responsible for the "bad" loans. When I was on the board of directors of a bank in

Humble, Texas, the first lesson I was taught as a new director was that banks generally make loans to people who do not need them. In other words, banks lend money to people with substantial collateral in land, real estate, or certificates of deposit.

What about mismanagement? If banks are mismanaged, obviously they can fail. But suppose the bank is properly managed, can it still fail? Of course. As the "Doom" experiment demonstrates, it makes no difference how much collateral the borrowers have. For some people to succeed, others must fail due to the inherent shortage of money to repay interest when new money is created as loans. The deficit situation is only compounded by new loans, not cured. It is important to note that when client borrowers suffer financial failure, some banks might also fail. Mismanagement can be a factor, but it is a minimal one. No bank president wants to lose his job, but when profits are not being generated, the first one to get blamed is the bank's president or the chief executive officer. No one realizes that the true reason for failures is built into the debt-dominant money system.

What about "bad times"? Bad times are not a cause of bank failures; they are only a symptom of a shortage of debt-free money in the economic system.

If bad loans, mismanagement, and bad times are not sufficient reasons for bank failure, then why do they fail? From the business cycle demonstrated in Exhibit 12, it is logical to assume that banks make more loans at the start of the expansion phase. During such a phase, interest rates are going up, and banks are willing to make more loans because they can earn more money from higher interest rates. Most of the time, banks make loans only when they are assured of more than adequate collateral in the form of real, tangible wealth.

Let us assume that at the midpoint of the expansion phase someone goes to the bank to borrow money for a house valued at $100,000. The bank is going great guns since the economy is in the expansion phase. The proposed homeowner puts down $5,000 and gets a $95,000 mortgage. He begins to make monthly payments on his home.

Three or four years later, the business cycle has already peaked, and the economy begins to contract because of a shortage of money in the economic arena. During the contraction phase, businesses begin to fail, bankruptcies occur, and people lose their jobs. Our homeowner loses his job. He can no longer afford to make monthly payments on his home. The bank forecloses, and because we are moving toward the bottom of the contraction phase in the business cycle, known as a recession, prices in certain segments of the economy fall. Let us assume that the real estate segment is affected and that the prices of homes plummet.

The home that was bought by the homeowner for $100,000 is now appraised at $50,000. By law, the bank cannot keep the home on its books for longer than three months. Let's say the homeowner still owes the bank $93,000 of his $95,000 debt, and the bank is able to sell the foreclosed home for $43,000. The difference between what the bank sold the house for and what the homeowner owed the bank totals $50,000. What does the bank do with this $50,000 loss? Although the bank created the $100,000 to finance the initial purchase out of thin air, can it write off the $50,000 deficiency? Yes, the bank writes it off from its real earned income, *but not from the created dollars.*

When the bank writes off the deficiency created by this transaction from real earned income, it thus diminishes its capital assets. In a recessionary period many people lose their jobs, and banks end up with many foreclosed properties and products on their hands. Thus, their capital shrinks.

If the property owners have other assets, banks may file deficiency lawsuits against them. In this parasitic money system, banks should not be allowed to file deficiency lawsuits against victims of foreclosed properties and products. Non-recourse loan provisions do prevent this action of course, but such loans are rarely approved by banks.

If you strip away the cobwebs, it becomes apparent that bank failures, like other business failures, are a direct consequence of our debt-dominant or all-debt money system. Mismanagement of a bank and bad loans are only a small part of the failure equation used by the hierarchy of our debt-dominant money system to divert public attention from the real cause of bank failures—the all-debt monetary system and its evil consequences: inflation, recessions, depressions, bankruptcies, foreclosures, and involuntary unemployment.

With this careful explanatory progression in this and the preceding chapters, I have demonstrated that the majority of the woes of humankind as related to economic adversity comes down to one major flaw in our monetary system . . . *the lack of debt-free money.* If all money is created as debt to be repaid at interest, funds that would otherwise be used to activate the production of goods and services are removed from the money supply in the form of interest payments to the money creators.

In chapter 11, I will diagrammatically demonstrate how economic recessions and depressions and all their nasty consequences can be prevented once and for all with some expedient action over the next several years. This "cure" will put an end to the continual exploitation of the productive elements of society. You will see how the solution can wipe out income tax and most other taxes, including the death and estate taxes that are so burdensome on the families of industrious and productive people.

This cure, with one fair sweep, will also wipe out the Internal Revenue Service and allow you to keep what you are willing and able to work for. Think hard, long, and passionately about this. Who could object to the abolishment of taxes and the IRS?

Chapter 10

Jewels in the English Channel

It is absurd to say that our country can issue thirty million dollars in bonds but not thirty million dollars in currency. Both are promises to pay. But one promise fattens the usurers, and the other helps the people.

Thomas Edison

Many people, including Thomas Edison who had no training as an economist, recognize that our money system is quite out-of-date. The present financial system suits only those who run it; those who control the purse strings exercise a major element of control over a nation. As current news reports attest, whole nations flounder in debt of untold trillions. This debt, however, reflects the goods and services in the marketplace—the money loaned would be without purchasing power if it was not backed by goods and services.

Surely with all our brainpower we can devise a system whereby money can be issued as required without having to resort to debt or usury. In fact, it has already been done. In Austria in a town called Wörgl, there is a bridge with a plaque prominently affixed to it. This plaque commemorates that the bridge was built by debt-free, locally created money. There was a similar issuance of money in Swanenkirchen, Bavaria. Both towns were transformed temporarily from poverty-ridden hamlets into prosperous communities by the simple and expedient issuance of debt-free money. Unfortunately, both were prevented from issuing additional money by their respective governments when those governments were pressured by private banking interests.

The Social Credit government in Alberta was also prevented from issuing its own currency by the Bank of Canada and the Ottawa government. The Alberta "Bill of Rights," a masterpiece of creative policy designed to give the citizens of Alberta complete economic freedom, has been declared *ultra vires* and similarly rejected by Ottawa.

Let us now focus on Guernsey, a small but beautiful island well-favored by nature in beauty and natural resources and by that most uncommon of human attributes, common sense.

Constitutional Position of the Channel Islands

The Channel Islands, of which the Bailiwick of Guernsey forms a part, occupy an unusual position in Her Majesty's possessions. They are not part of the United Kingdom, nor are they sovereign states or colonies. In the British Nationality Act of 1948, they are distinguished by the reference to "A Citizen of the United Kingdom, Islands and Colonies."

They maintain insular legislatures, judiciaries, and executives, but the United Kingdom is responsible for Guernsey's defense and international relations. Their constitutional position is a direct result of a number of historical circumstances, beginning with their integration into the Duchy of Normandy in the tenth and eleventh centuries and the relationship between the duchy and kingdom created by the Norman conquest and colonization of England after the Battle of Hastings.

When continental Normandy was overrun by the king of France in 1204, the islands remained in the hands of the king of England, who continued to govern them in his capacity as duke of Normandy until he surrendered the title in 1259. Five years earlier, however, King Henry III had granted them to his eldest son and heir, the future King Edward I, and, ". . . no one, by reason of this grant made to the said Edward may have any claim to the said lands . . . but that they should remain to the Kings of England in their entirety forever."

The effect was that the islands were "annexed to the Crown." That is to say, whoever was the lawful king of England was by that fact alone the lawful ruler of the Channel Islands; but the islands were not incorporated into the kingdom of England then or at any subsequent time.

In French law, however, the islands remained a parcel of the kingdom of France (which was clearly acknowledged in the Treaty of 1259) until some later point in the Middle Ages that has not yet been determined by historians or constitutional lawyers. Since their ecclesiastical, trading, and even personal relations with Normandy remained very close until well into modern times, the fact that they have remained a possession of the English Crown owes much to their continued loyalty.

Though he had surrendered the ducal title, then, the king of England continued to rule the islands as though he were Duke of Normandy, observing their laws, customs, and liberties. These local rights were later confirmed by the charters of successive sovereigns, which secured for the islands their own judiciaries and thus freedom from the process of English courts and other important privileges of which the islands are justly proud. Although expressed in somewhat different terms in different ages, this sovereignty has remained the essence of the relationship between the islands and the Crown to the present day.

After the separation of the islands from Normandy and its administration, the local institutions were largely molded from local initiative to meet changing circumstances, until their present constitutions evolved. The evolution, however, did not at any time involve amalgamation with or subjection to the government of the United Kingdom, and even today the islands' link with the United Kingdom and the remainder of the Commonwealth is through the sovereign as latter-day successor to the dukes of Normandy.

The Channel Islands consist of two bailiwicks, the Bailiwick of Guernsey and the Bailiwick of Jersey, each independent of each other and having separate legislatures, judiciaries, and executives. The Bailiwick of Guernsey comprises the islands of Guernsey, Alderney, and Sark and the dependencies of Herm and Jethou, all of which are inhabited. The total population is about sixty-five thousand, and the islands enjoy a prosperity much higher than that of the British Isles and higher than that of France. (Guernsey lies eight miles off the French coast and during World War II was occupied by German troops.)

The First Steps to Prosperity

At the beginning of the nineteenth century, just after the Napoleonic Wars, the Island of Guernsey was in poor economic condition. Apart from the natural beauty and pleasant climate, there was precious little to attract visitors to the island or to keep inhabitants from emigrating to the mainland of western Europe or to the United Kingdom. The deep roads were nothing more than cart tracks only four feet, six inches wide that became swift, muddy rivers between steep banks during heavy rains.

The town of St. Peters Port, the capital city, was ill-paved and unattractive. There was not a vehicle of any kind for hire on the island. There was no trade nor hope of employment for the poor and unemployed. The sea was rapidly encroaching the land, washing away large tracts of it due to the sorry state of the dykes. The state debt of £19,137 sterling bore an annual interest charge of £2,390, and annual revenues amounted to only £3,000. Thus while vast sums of money were required to save the land from the encroaching sea, only £610 of revenue was available for such expenditures. The dyke project alone was estimated to cost over £10,000. The government faced a dilemma. Their expenditures would run into the tens of thousands of pounds, and their annual revenue amounted to £610, not enough funds even to start the project.

How was this problem solved? In 1815, a committee was appointed to examine how to improve the public market, which then provided neither cover nor shelter. The committee found that further taxation on the poor islands was not only out of the question, it was impossible. The alternative, that is, borrowing money from banks, would incur debt charges of a high interest rate, which the government could not afford. It was clear that even if the needed funds could be borrowed, there was scant possibility that the debt could ever be retired, even though interest charges might be met.

After grave deliberation, the committee made a historic recommendation in 1816—that property be acquired and a closed market be erected. The expenses would be met by issuing state notes to the value of £6,000. (How most nobly does man create when his adversities are greatest!)

The arguments put forward in favor of this plan are most interesting, as shown by this extract from the committee report: "The committee recommends that the expense should be met by the issue of states notes of one pound sterling to the value of £6,000 . . . and that these notes will be available not only for the payment of the new market, but also for Torteval Church, roads to construct, and other expenses of the States . . . when one considers that the banks already have their notes in circulation for more than £50,000, whereas it is now proposed to restrict the States' issue to a mere £6,000. . . . "

The argument was also put forth that the issue would provide a permanent revenue to the states, sufficient not only to provide for construction of the market but also to create an amortization fund to extinguish the outstanding debt of the states.

These proposals, however, were not implemented until later in the same year when the first issue of states' notes was authorized for a sum of £4,000 for coast preservation works, the Torteval Church, and Jerbourg Monument. These notes were issued subject to redemption in three stages— April 1817, October 1817, and April 1818—and not for reissue. The committee's report recommending the issue stated: "In this manner, without increasing the States' debt, it will be possible to finish these works, leaving sufficient money in the exchequer for other needs."

It was not until 1820, after another aborted attempt in 1819, that the committee was successful in its attempt to finance the building of a new market. It was at last given authority to issue states' notes for that purpose to a value of £4,500, redeemable in ten years out of import duties and revenue from the various market shops.

HOW THE MARKETS WERE BUILT

In 1820 the States agreed to build a covered Market for £5,500. As they had £1,000 in hand, 4,500 notes of £1 were issued on the security of a small tax on spirituous liquors. The work was undertaken and the Market completed and opened in 1822.

Each of the 36 shops yielded £5 in rent. As soon as the £180 was received each year, 180 States' notes were burnt. The 4,500 notes would have taken too long to destroy at this rate but the States also paid into the Market Fund £300 per annum derived from tax on wines coming into the Island

£30 of this were set aside for running repairs and £270 went towards the extinction of more paper notes.

At the end of ten years not one of the notes issued to pay for the building was left, no interest had been paid upon them and there was a steady income of £180.

The huge granite structure still stands; it has a dark exterior countenance, but the interior is bright and clean with various booths offering a wide variety of produce, vegetables, and meats. At one entrance and at another exit are two framed notices describing how the market was built with notes issued by the states interest-free to citizens.

This interest-free issue of £4,500 for construction of the market was quickly followed by others, and in 1821 the number of notes in circulation was increased on the committee's recommendation to £10,000. From the point of view of both the public and the states' finances, this method was most advantageous for meeting debts. Indeed, the public seemed to realize this fact, and far from being adverse to taking the notes, they sought them out eagerly. The notes, while they were in circulation, earned interest for the states' Treasury, and the more interest the Treasury collected, the less the Treasury needed through taxation. The market was opened in October of 1822 and has operated continuously ever since.

In 1824, a further £5,000 was authorized for the market, and in 1826 the issue was increased to a total of £20,000 to erect Elizabeth College and certain parochial schools. This year also the first States' of Guernsey five-pound notes appeared in public circulation.

By 1829, the states' notes issue in circulation exceeded £48,000; by 1837, the grand total was over £55,000. Eminent men of those times stated that without the issue of states' notes, important public works such as roads and buildings could not possibly have been completed. By means of the states' issue, however, not only were these works accomplished, but the island was not a penny the poorer from interest charges. Indeed, the improvements had stimulated a flow of visitors to the island, and with the increased trade, the island enjoyed a newfound prosperity.

Temporary Setbacks

It is a truism that you can't please everybody all the time, and this truth came to bear on the Guernsey States' notes issue. During the first ten years of the experiment, there was no opposition. In 1826, however, certain individuals made representations to the privy counsel in England, complaining that the states had no right to issue states' notes in excess of their annual income without royal consent. An explanation was demanded by the Privy Counsel and was supplied by the states' financial committee. *The arguments pointing out the innumerable good to the public resulting from the issuance of states' notes were so compelling that the Privy Counsel closed the matter once and for all.*

The most serious threat to the Guernsey experiment, though, came from the expected quarter—from the two private banks on the island, namely the Old Bank and the Commercial Bank founded in 1827 and 1830, respectively. These private institutions flooded the island with paper money. Fearing their own notes would be prejudiced, the states appointed a committee to confer with representatives of the two banks. What transpired is difficult to understand, but eventually it was the states who withdrew £15,000 of their notes in circulation, not the banks. By any stretch of the imagination, such an action on the part of the states could not have been rationalized. In addition, the states agreed to limit their future issue to £40,000. No light can be shed on the reasons for this decision; there are no records other than the bare facts. This agreement remained in force until 1914, when states' notes in circulation amounted to £41,206.

During all this time, only one forgery had been attempted, and, since it was very crude, it was immediately detected. As a consequence, though, it was deemed necessary to withdraw the entire issue, which was replaced by a new issue of "Greenbacks."

Full Steam Ahead

For over seventy years the position of Guernsey remained static, with a limited states' issue at £40,000, but in 1914 the states were able to turn the table on the private banks and once more issue money according to their own needs in the marketplace. This change came about because of the restrictions imposed on the banks during the First World War—demand for money was enormous, but banks were prohibited from issuing more than the amount of their money already in circulation. The states, however, were under no such limitation. They made such good use of their opportunity that by the end of the war in 1918, the states' issue had risen to £142,000.

Since then, Guernsey has not looked back. Her notes issue has risen in measure with her prosperity, and in 1958 there were £542,765 in circulation. About that time, the local Guernsey banks amalgamated with English banking concerns, and private bank notes disappeared. States' notes circulated side by side with British notes and were fully redeemable in British Treasury notes.

On Guernsey there is greater demand for States' notes; no sane citizen wishes to have his taxes increased to pay interest on debt. In 1937 the states' note money, about £175,000, cost the states only £450 for printing and handling. A loan of the same dimensions would have cost about £11,383 in annual interest charges. Can you blame Guernsey taxpayers for preferring their own money, since under their sensible system they pay minimal income tax?

During the experiment in Guernsey from about 1817 to about 1958, there was at no time a threat of inflation from the creation of states' notes. At all times the states were careful to issue notes according to public requirements. Any visitor to Guernsey is immediately impressed by the significant difference in prices between the island and the mainland of Great Britain. Thanks to low taxation and import duties, Guernsey citizens enjoy low prices, have high levels of income, and a high standard of living. Guernsey leaves worries about inflation to the debt-ridden countries like the

United States, Great Britain, Canada, Japan, West Germany, Brazil, Argentina, Venezuela, Mexico, and eastern Europe. Early in 1990, culminating more than seven years of research for this book, I made a personal visit to Guernsey with a friend who has collaborated with me in preparation of this work. My research had indicated that Guernsey enjoyed a unique monetary history that had led to extraordinary success, but I felt compelled to collect some additional data.

On March 4, 1990, at 7 P.M., we boarded a British Airways DC 10 at Houston Intercontinental Airport and took off for Guernsey. At Gatwick Airport, London, we discovered there were several flights daily to and from Guernsey, and we were able to advance our schedule by some eight hours. We arrived in Guernsey at 1 P.M. local time the following day and were settled into our hotel, the Duke of Richmond, by mid-afternoon.

We were in Guernsey at the invitation of the States Treasurer of Guernsey, Michael J. Brown, who graciously consented to an in-depth interview the following afternoon. The next day, I walked into the downtown area of St. Peters Port, the capital city of the island. I wanted to see the granite building that opened as the public market in 1822, having been constructed with interest-free money issued by the state. Gazing at the imposing structure, I was struck by the wisdom of the people responsible for the issuance of the states' notes. As I looked over the building, I asked about the plaques that explained how the structure was constructed. The citizens were extremely helpful as they located the framed explanations.

While we were outside taking photographs, citizens gathered to offer information. Streets were narrow, very clean, and there were signs of prosperity everywhere. I concluded my examination of the market and went back to the hotel to prepare for my meeting with the states treasurer.

At 1:30 P.M. I was ushered into Mr. Brown's office. He confirmed the information I had previously discovered about Guernsey—that it had £13 million of states' notes circulating on the island. The Guernsey notes are only spendable in Guernsey—my five-pound Guernsey note was rebuffed at the Hilton Gatwick Hotel the next day—but are fully redeemable in English pound notes and coins at one of the many money-changing booths at the airport.

Over the past three years (1987-1989), there has been an increase of 40 percent in the real money supply. Currently the inflation rate in Guernsey is running about 9 percent annually, an apparition caused by lower prices in Guernsey and the fact that most goods are imported. For example, gasoline costs about one pound at the petrol pump at Guernsey stations, while the price tag is two pounds in England. A ten-pence tax increase on gasoline in England translates into a 5 percent tax hike, while in Guernsey the price is escalated by 10 percent. There is no value added tax in Guernsey, but this broad-based tax is factored into the cost of imported goods from the Common Market countries, thus skewing the rate of inflation upwards.

The fact that the money supply in Guernsey has increased 40 percent in real terms without runaway inflation is a strong argument against the traditional explanation—that inflation is caused by "too much money chasing too few goods."

Mr. Brown pointed out that unemployment on the island is zero. He showed us a newspaper with hundreds of ads offering jobs of every description. Guernsey opens its job market to foreign labor, but only up to eight months at a time.

We were impressed with the number of cars on the island. We were told that there were about forty-four thousand cars and that the average home is priced at £140,000. The standard of living in Guernsey is quite high, but consumer prices are about one-half that of the United Kingdom, and since 1960 the income tax rate has been a constant 20 percent. This is due in part to the fact that Guernsey *earns* about six million pounds *interest income* on its states' issue yearly, while all debt-money countries like the United States continue to *pay interest.*

Finance is the leading industry on the island, with tourism and agriculture following in that order. Banks are everywhere and are sometimes located right next door to one another, often three in a row. Tourism is the second leading industry, and the island has a large yacht harbor with yachts from all over the world. Agriculture, called "growing" by the locals, is carried out mainly in greenhouses, which are among the most noticeable structures on the island as you approach it by air.

During the meeting, I asked if they ever had a shortage of money to finance public projects? "No," replied Mr. Brown, "We always have a surplus of funds." At that point he brought out a publication to show the status of the island's finances. It showed that the island government never operates in the red and that their surplus funds earn income in the form of interest.

After a four-hour session, we concluded our interview with Mr. Brown. Riding back to the hotel, I reflected again on what I had heard. Guernsey and Jersey issue states' notes according to the needs of the public, while the rest of the world endures debt, hunger, and starvation. Guernsey and Jersey are two gems that stand out as shining exceptions to a globe wallowing in economic chaos. I thought about how much the Third World countries, the Eastern Bloc countries breaking away from communism, the USSR itself, and, most of all, the United States with a public debt approaching $4 trillion, could learn from these two independent countries in the English Channel.

Some may argue that debt-free money might work on a small island but is not applicable to a large economy such as in the United States. Such arguments are nonsense. One over two equals one-half, and so does 500,000 over 1,000,000. The size of the numbers may be different, but the ratio is the same; and it is the ratio of debt-free money to debt money that is important.

The world in which we live is prey to some puzzling contradictions. On the one hand, scientific progress is mind boggling. Not only have we split the atom, thereby releasing the forces of the universe, we have opened up new vistas in space for mankind that even Jules Verne or H. G. Wells would not have envisioned. The industrial revolution has arrived long since, and the use of automation is here to stay. Despite all these achievements, we are compelled to do dull and degrading work that could easily be carried out by machines, but no work means no wages, no food, no clothing, and no shelter.

Our desire for security and the "good things" in life are translated into demands for full employment, no matter how unnecessary. It is unfashionable nowadays to refer to poverty in the midst of plenty, but alas, poverty is an ever-present fact to undernourished retired persons depending on their shrinking social security checks, the sick, and poorly paid or unemployed workers.

The gulf stretches between what we are and what we could be. We have attained mastery of many elements on earth, but we continue to endure poverty and exploitation despite all our advancements.

You would think that a planet abundant in natural resources and more than an adequate labor force could easily convert those natural resources into all the wealth you could possibly use or want. Obviously, this is not the case, so something must be wrong, terribly wrong.

Money is the catalyst that activates production of the labor force. Money is also necessary for the transfer of goods and services between producers, retailers, and consumers. There is nothing wrong with money, but there is something gravely wrong with our money systems. Although many people in many countries—including the governments of such countries—realize that there are grave problems with their money systems, nothing is being done to correct the problems. Of course, the present financial system suits the people running it, and those who control the purse strings control the nation. It suits the banking system to retain their power by keeping the money stock scarce. It is strange that with so many goods for sale in the shops, there seems to be a shortage of ready cash. Were it not for the dynamic process of debt creation such as installment purchase and personal loans, our economy would soon be on the rocks—it would flounder on a surfeit of unsold goods.

Debt in the postwar world is a commonplace word. Debt is more common than bread—note that most of the Third World countries have debt but have no bread. Surely we can devise a system whereby money can be issued as required to benefit all humankind without resorting to debt or usury.

Chapter 11

The Solution

No more cunning a plot was ever devised against the intelligence, the freedom, the happiness and the honest virtue of the American people than the national debt and the debt-dominant money system.

As demonstrated previously, in an all-debt or debt-dominant money system it is mathematically and physically impossible to repay the aggregate debt, for only money representing the principal is ever created. The interest that must be repaid along with the principal debt is never created. For some people to repay their principal and interest, their interest must come from the principal created for other people's debt. A deficit in the aggregate money supply thus occurs, making it impossible for other debtors to repay their principal, much less principal and interest.

This design error in our monetary system grew out of the goldsmith money system, which simply evolved without being systematically designed. A logically designed system that eliminates this inherent error will work to the advantage of all Americans and all humankind.

To correct the error, we must first understand it. If one does not understand the problem, then assessing the solution becomes impossible. We do not want a "quick fix" to alleviate the symptoms of inflation, recession, economic depression, bankruptcies, foreclosures, and involuntary unemployment, but rather a lasting solution that will eradicate the problems in our present-day system. Quick fixes have been attempted for centuries, all of which were doomed to eventual failure because they dealt only with the symptoms and not the cause of the problem. I target here the disease, *the all-debt monetary system itself.*

The Problem

The Mayflower arrived at Plymouth, Massachusetts, in 1620. It carried the first mighty vanguard to arrive on these shores from across the Atlantic. During these early times, bartering was widespread. Settlers bartered their produce and goods with each other. Little money was seen in America during the early years of colonization. Only some gold and silver coin brought over from the Old World was used to facilitate trade between the people of the colonies of Maine, Connecticut, Rhode Island, and New Hampshire.

Black and white shells, otherwise known as Indian wampum, represented certain values among Indians, and they found their way into the hands of the colonists. They soon learned they could use it as a medium of exchange very satisfactorily. The colonies also stamped gold and silver coins and put them into circulation.

After a time it became apparent that trade was being strangled because of insufficient money, or something to use for money. A circulating medium called "Colonial Scrip" was thus born, authorized by the governors of the various colonies. With this release of purchasing power, great prosperity came to the colonies since there was an abundance of produce and goods available.

Today in our all-debt money system, money is created by the privately owned Federal Reserve banks, commercial banks, and thrift institutions. Almost all the money is created as debt and then lent either to the government or to the private sector.

In Exhibit 13, the upper sphere represents the privately owned banks, and the lower sphere represents the economic arena, designated as "E.A." Assume that for a particular year the government borrows $1000 at 10 percent annual interest from privately owned banks. Let us also assume that during the same year the private sector borrows $3000 at 10 percent annual interest. I have chosen these numbers because government—federal, state and local—has accounted for about 25 percent of total annual spending in recent years in the United States.

Given $1000 spent by government and $3000 spent by the private sector, a total of $4000 has been spent into the economy during the year. If this $4000 were repaid at the end of the year, leaving at the exit marked "principal," then $4000 drains out of the economy and returns to the banks. The M1 will then be zero. However, the interest due the banks is 10 percent of the $4000 or $400. Of course, the M1 in the economy is now zero, and there is no money to go through the interest exit to the banks. *The interest charge thus accumulates exponentially as debt each year.* The patent impossibility of an all-debt or debt-dominant monetary system is apparent in this diagram.

If the private sector repaid its debt of $3000 at 10 percent interest, the banks would receive $3300, leaving only

EXHIBIT 13
PROBLEM
PRIVATELY OWNED BANKS ARE:
FEDERAL RESERVE BANKS, COMMERCIAL BANKS & THRIFTS

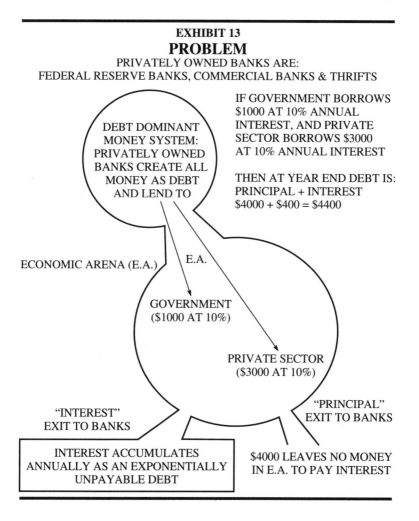

DEBT DOMINANT
MONEY SYSTEM:
PRIVATELY OWNED
BANKS CREATE ALL
MONEY AS DEBT
AND LEND TO

IF GOVERNMENT BORROWS
$1000 AT 10% ANNUAL
INTEREST, AND PRIVATE
SECTOR BORROWS $3000
AT 10% ANNUAL INTEREST

THEN AT YEAR END DEBT IS:
PRINCIPAL + INTEREST
$4000 + $400 = $4400

ECONOMIC ARENA (E.A.)

E.A.

GOVERNMENT
($1000 AT 10%)

PRIVATE SECTOR
($3000 AT 10%)

"INTEREST"
EXIT TO BANKS

"PRINCIPAL"
EXIT TO BANKS

INTEREST ACCUMULATES
ANNUALLY AS AN EXPONENTIALLY
UNPAYABLE DEBT

$4000 LEAVES NO MONEY
IN E.A. TO PAY INTEREST

$700 in the economy. It is thus impossible for the government to repay its debt of $1000 plus 10 percent interest, or $1100. Or, vice versa, if the public sector repaid its total debt of $1100, the private sector would be short the necessary funds to meet its obligations. Because there is no debt-free money in the economy, it is impossible for all borrowers to repay their total debt. To solve this dilemma, we need to spend some debt-free money into circulation.

Who should have the right to spend such debt-free money? It would be patently unfair for the handful in the private sector who now create money out of thin air to create and spend debt-free money into the economy. It is more reasonable to expect that this debt-free expenditure should be made by the national Treasury for the benefit of all the people in America. *This pivotal point of monetary reform will cure the ills of our current flawed system.*

Law and Money

In past civilizations, many different objects have served as money. Whatever we use as money does not have to be intrinsically valuable. But the money system in use should maintain reasonable purchasing stability over time.

In the United States today, citizens pay considerable taxes in one form or another on a large part of their earnings. Whatever they use to pay taxes becomes money. Today, the Internal Revenue Service accepts coins, Federal Reserve notes, and checkbook money in payment of taxes. If the United States Congress should decide that it will accept canceled stamps on envelopes that are issued by the U.S. Post Office, all these canceled stamps would then acquire purchasing power as money. Obviously, then, what becomes money is provided by the *law* and not by the whimsical urge of any one person or group of people. *Law* is what makes money acceptable as money, and to be money, it must be acceptable for payment of debts and taxes.

Why Not Return to the Gold Standard?

For some curious reason rooted in antiquity, gold has been the goddess of confidence and false hope. The "gold standard" and "gold redeemable currency" are terminologies that have been around for a long time, but very few understand what they mean.

When a nation is on a "gold standard," the national government has simply agreed with the international banking industry that it will buy, sell, and trade in gold at a fixed and guaranteed price for a specific weight and purity of the metal.

On the other hand, currency that is "gold redeemable" is totally different and has been around for thousands of years, long before the "gold standard" was invented. In the chapter entitled *"Banking and the Goldsmiths,"* I explained that the goldsmith of old was probably the best known "promisor and redeemer" of paper currency. The gold receipts he issued were transmuted into currency over a period of time.

The goldsmith promised to redeem all the gold receipts he issued, lent, and invested, even though he could not redeem more than a fraction of them. He began issuing receipts far in excess of his cache of gold when he learned that the metal was rarely redeemed. The modern banker, on the other hand, never promises to redeem his bank-created checkbook money for anything. Even the Federal Reserve notes, the cash currency that we currently use in this country, cannot be redeemed for anything except for another Federal Reserve note or for coins—nickels, dimes, and so on.

After 1764 when the debt-money system was introduced in America, one could not redeem all one's money for gold. Only cash currency was ever redeemable in gold. Checkbook money, which comprised a greater part of the money supply, could never be redeemed in gold. And even cash currency—the currency issued by the Federal Reserve banks in the form of Federal Reserve notes" has not been redeemable for gold since 1968.

Proponents of a return to the gold standard, namely academia, economists, elected officials, and a veritable myriad of money reform experts, should know that the gold standard in the United States never prevented the financial panics and catastrophes we have endured in the past. The gold standard was adopted in the United States in 1900, and through the twelve Federal Reserve bank corporations established in 1913, the United States became a full-fledged gold standard member. It was under this gold standard that the United States economy was maneuvered into a severe economic recession in 1920, and in 1929 the United States experienced the worst economic depression in its history. Obviously a gold standard does not prevent economic recessions or depressions.

It is historically documented that the so-called gold standard in operation in this country did not prevent average retail food prices from rising more than 160 percent between 1900 and 1929. Sixteen percent of the labor force was thrown out of work in the 1920-1921 recession, and in the 1929 depression thousands of businesses and industries were wiped out as a result of forced bankruptcies and foreclosures. The gold standard did not prevent this wrenching economic perdition, and it did not prevent 21 percent of the work force, men and women who were willing and able to work, from being forced into involuntary unemployment between 1931 and 1935.

If we did go back to the gold standard, then our money supply would be dependent on the supply of gold. Unless additional gold was found and mined, we would not be able to increase the money supply in our economy, despite the demand for money in the marketplace.

The supply of money should meet the demand for it in the economy. Money not only activates output, but it measures the output of the productive elements of society. It is the lifeblood of commerce. If its availability is dependent upon a commodity that must be mined from the earth, and if there is a shortage of that commodity, a shortage in the money supply will occur despite the need for an expanded money supply.

The most crucial reason why the United States should not return to the gold standard is because it cannot.

"Gold certificates, which are valued at $42.22 per Troy ounce of gold, are a liability of the Treasury, and are issued to the Federal Reserve by the Treasury against its gold holding. The certificates represent a Federal Reserve claim on the assets of the Treasury, for which the Treasury has received a counterpart deposit in its account with the Federal Reserve. All gold held by the Treasury has been monetized in this fashion."[1]

Translated, this means that although the gold may be physically present in the vaults of the national Treasury, all this gold has been mortgaged to the Federal Reserve and therefore belongs to the Federal Reserve. Exhibit 14 details the condition of all Federal Reserve banks combined. One can see here under "assets" that the gold certificate account totals $11.083 billion—and remember, the Federal Reserve System is privately owned!

To corroborate the fact that the United States Treasury no longer owns any gold, one can look at the *United States Treasury Bulletin* of December 1976. From this publication it is clear that there is no more gold in the United States Treasury gold account. A footnote states, "As of December

EXHIBIT 14
DETAILED STATEMENT OF CONDITION OF ALL
FEDERAL RESERVE BANKS COMBINED.
December 31, 1986

Thousands of dollars

ASSETS

Gold Certificate Amount **11,083,947**
Special drawing rights certificate account 5,018,000
Coin 485,827

Loans and Securities
    Loans to depository Institutions 1,564,797
    Federal Agency obligations bought outright 7,829,312
    Held under repurchase agreement 2,313,535
    Bought outright
    Bills 103,774,920
    Notes 68,125,600
    Bonds 25,723,814
    Total bought outright 197,624,334
    Held under re-purchase agreement 13,691,465
    Total Securities 211,315,799
    Total loans and securities 223,023,443

Items in Process of Collection
    Transit items 8,063,084
    Other items in process of collection 2,211,741
    Total items in process of collection 10,274,825

Bank premises
    Land 105,638
    Buildings (including vaults) .452,363
    Building machinery and eqt. .157,448
    Construction equipment 127,236
    Total bank premises 737,047
    Less depreciation allowance 182,516 554,531
    Bank premises, net 660,169

Other assets
    Furniture and equipment 515,885
    Less depreciation 249,460
    Total furniture and equipment, net 266,425
    Denominated in foreign currencies 9,474,797
    Interest accrued 2,601,442
    Premium on securities 1,206,675
    Due from Fed. Dep. Ins. Corp. 2,904,299
    Overdrafts 190,096
    Prepaid expenses 26,159
    Suspense account 17,483
    Real estate acquired for banking-house purposes 6,368
    Other 126,488

    Total other assets 16,820,232

    Total assets 267,366,443

REF: 73rd Annual Report of: Board of Governors of the Federal Reserve System-1986, pg. 222.

9, 1974, gold certificates have been issued to the Federal Reserve against all of the gold owned by the United States Government."[2]

So, to those who advocate a return to the gold standard, I say, "Forget it." The United States owns no gold! All gold now stored in the U.S. Treasury vaults belongs to the privately owned Federal Reserve banks and has been so owned for more than a decade.

A Mathematical Approach

Total debt in the U.S. as of April 1987 amounted to $7.6 trillion. At the same time, the money supply, M1, was $730.5 billion.[3] You don't have to be an Einstein to figure out that, if the money supply is $730.5 billion and the total debt in the economy is $7.6 trillion, it is impossible to repay the total debt without either reducing the debt or increasing the money supply.

One can argue that the value of assets in the United States is far in excess of the total debt. That is true, but regardless of the value of the asset, you still require money to transact business unless you return to the barter system. You cannot go to the bank and make interest payments with bushels of corn, wheat, cattle, or a piece of land. A bank debt repayment requires money. Money in the United States is currency, coins, and checkbook money, not hard assets.

A billion dollars worth of assets, will not buy you a hamburger at Burger King. In fact, the single place you can repay bank debt with hard assets is in a bankruptcy court!

It is not difficult to perceive what has been happening to our economy. Weekly, dozens of businesses fail because of a lack of money in the marketplace. Bankruptcies, bank failures, and foreclosures all result from a shortage of money in the economy. When there is a shortage of money, the labor force cannot earn adequate money, even if they are willing and able to work for it.

Money is based on numbers and mathematics, a pure science since it obeys specific laws. By observing the basic laws of mathematics, one can design a monetary system in which the purchasing power of our unit of currency remains reasonably stable. We can apply mathematical standards that deal in absolutes and avoid economic standards that deal with dynamic, changing relationships and forecasts that have been consistently wrong.

I have discussed this point with many economists, and most have concurred that economics is not a science—a social science, perhaps, but not a pure science. Empirical evaluations of complex, dynamic relationships form the basis of economic theory. If economics is not a pure science, then it is logical to conclude that economists are not pure scientists. But if money is based on numbers, which is a true science, then why has the preponderance of government effort been directed toward solving a scientific problem without the aid of pure scientists?

Monetary scientists who understand the problems of an all-debt monetary system are needed to solve the unstable monetary systems of the world. These will be people who, by virtue of training, can examine an effect, analyze it, and work backwards to identify its cause in our economic system. They are inductive analysts who operate in a conclusive, cause-effect framework rather than drawing conclusions on the basis of historic data.

The Right to Create Money

Money is only a medium of exchange and should be considered a public utility. Its creation is for the benefit of all the citizens of a particular country and not for the benefit of only a handful of citizens. Money is the lifeblood of commerce and industry. Without money, there would be no economy, and civilization as we know it today would wither and die. Our society is much too complex to revert to the barter system.

Since money is the lifeblood of commerce and is for the benefit of all citizens of America, the big question is, *who should have the right to create it?* We live in a democracy in this country, and the majority of our citizens would agree that the right to create money should be in the hands of all the people; that is, the government should have this right. Since it is too cumbersome for each citizen to create his own money, the process of creating money should rest in the hands of the people who are elected to serve the citizens, the Congress. Checks and balances can be lawfully enacted to prevent Congressional abuse in the money creation process. We already have checks and balances in our government, and they seem to function quite well. Why should the public object to the government creating money? The greatest majority of the American citizenry already believes that the government creates our money.

According to the Constitution, the sovereign authority in America is the American people. Since the Congress is duly elected by the people it should be the right of Congress, through the national Treasury, to create money for the benefit of all the people. Not only should the national Treasury create money for the people, but *it should be the only creative source of money for the U.S. citizenry.* The national

Treasury must be the only authorized source of money in the United States.

The results of usury are not easily perceived due to the slowness of the cycle in which it operates. The cycle usually extends over several centuries and the resultant disasters may be witnessed only by one generation in many generations. To understand the sequence of events that leads to disaster, we must know history. Lending money at interest was the custom in ancient Egypt, Babylon, Persia, Greece, and Rome, and there is evidence that this pattern was always regarded as disastrous.

"Only about three percent of our money is in coins."[4] This portion of the money supply (M1) is the only one created by the U.S. government, a one-time creation. The other 97 percent of the M1, namely checkbook money and Federal Reserve notes, is continuously created by the privately owned Federal Reserve banks, the commercial banks, and the thrifts. The money created either by a computer entry or a bookkeeping entry on the ledgers of banks belongs to the banks that create the entries.

The banking industry is the only industry on the face of this planet that does not have to labor for or pay for its merchandising stock. The very merchandise the banking industry rents, money, is obtained at absolutely no cost to them. Can you think of anything more devastating and unfair to the productive elements of society? It is imperative we understand that it is only a matter of time before the money creators dispossess the productive elements of our society. Once we understand this, if we stand by and allow it to occur, we deserve our fate. Today the United States government has the ability to create a dollar's worth of bond and to give this bond to the privately owned Federal Reserve bank as collateral. The Federal Reserve then creates a dollar of checkbook money out of thin air, as a bookkeeping entry, and lends this newly created money to the federal government at a price, known as interest.

If the federal government can create a dollar's worth of bond, why can't it create the dollar bill directly? Instead of getting a Federal Reserve note, why not use a United States note or dollar? How can the entire American citizenry be duped into believing that the privately created Federal Reserve notes, not backed by anything, are more valuable than a United States note, issued by the American government and backed by the integrity of the whole citizenry of America.

The Federal Reserve Act of 1913 did not relinquish the power to create money to the privately owned Federal Reserve banks, commercial banks, or thrift institutions. It would require an amendment to Article 1, Section 8, Clause 5, of the Constitution to do so. But this part of our Constitution was never amended; it is still the law of the land.

What percentage of our elected officials today truly understand that Congress still has the right to create money? If they really do understand this, why do they allow a private corporation to create money out of thin air that they borrow at an interest charge that is passed along to United States taxpayers? There is neither rhyme nor reason in such an arrangement, which is the ultimate manifestation of the fundamental flaw plaguing our economy. It is also blatantly unfair to the productive elements of society upon which the health of our economy depends.

The Equitable Solution

The solution to this problem does not involve complex economic formulas, nor does it involve any abstruse mathematical concepts. It does involve common sense, simple arithmetic, and some basic honesty.

What we need to solve our cyclical problems such as inflation and recession is a metered amount of debt-free money injected into the economy. This money will compensate for the continuous withdrawal of money from the economy by the private sector to satisfy debt service on its borrowings. The cure is at once absurdly simple but profoundly sweeping.

Debt-free money as well as debt-money should be in balanced amounts in our economy. *The national Treasury should create all money in America—coins, currency, and checkbook money.* The private sector, corporations or individuals, should not be allowed to create money.

Banks should be in the business of banking and not in the business of money creation. Money creation should be in the hands of Congress only. Also, banks should only be allowed to lend money that actually exists—money they own, money on deposit, or money they borrow from the Treasury. In other words, banks should operate with a 100 percent reserve.

Banks should finance the needs of the private sector by borrowing from the national Treasury at a low interest rate and then lending out the borrowed funds at a higher interest rate to maintain a margin of profit, just like any other commercial enterprise. Lending by banks should include all consumer and commercial loans. Interest payments on consumer loans, of course, aren't passed on to produce inflation; only interest on commercial loans are passed on as a cost of doing business. The Federal Reserve banks should be owned by the national Treasury and not by commercial banks and thrift institutions, and they should create debt-free money for public expenditures. The Federal Reserve banks

EXHIBIT 15
SOLUTION
BALANCED MONEY SYSTEM:
NATIONAL TREASURY CREATES AND EXTINGUISHES ALL MONEY

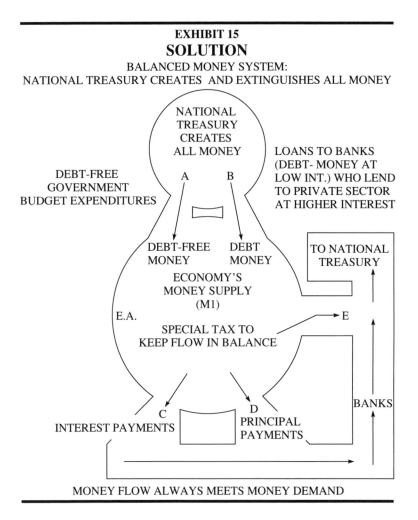

NATIONAL
TREASURY
CREATES
ALL MONEY

LOANS TO BANKS
(DEBT- MONEY AT
LOW INT.) WHO LEND
TO PRIVATE SECTOR
AT HIGHER INTEREST

DEBT-FREE
GOVERNMENT
BUDGET EXPENDITURES

A   B

DEBT-FREE   DEBT
MONEY   MONEY

TO NATIONAL
TREASURY

ECONOMY'S
MONEY SUPPLY
(M1)

E.A.

E

SPECIAL TAX TO
KEEP FLOW IN BALANCE

C
INTEREST PAYMENTS

D
PRINCIPAL
PAYMENTS

BANKS

MONEY FLOW ALWAYS MEETS MONEY DEMAND

should also have a certain degree of independence to restrain governmental abuse of the money creation process.

Not only should the national Treasury be the only creative source of all money, but it should maintain a balance
in the monetary system. The national Treasury should moni-
tor the monetary system to make sure that the annual infu-

Debt Virus

sion of debt-free budget expenditures is equal to or greater than the annual interest payments to banks by the private sector for all types of loans. *The only way the national Treasury will be able to do this task is for it to serve as the sole clearing house for all checks and electronic transfers of money.*

EXHIBIT 16
MONEY FLOW IN BALANCED MONEY SYSTEM

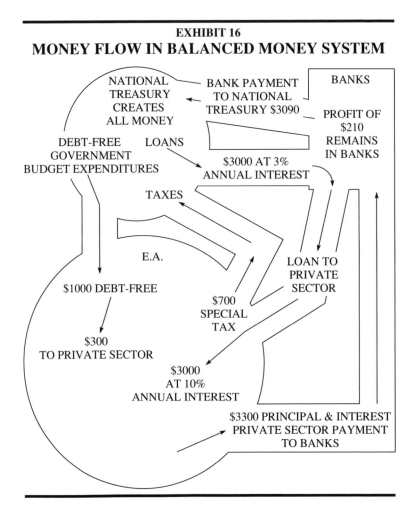

Using the same numbers as in the previous example, suppose the national Treasury created and spent $1000 of debt-free money into the economy for public expenditures.

Now assume that the banks borrow $3000 from the national Treasury at a 3 percent annual interest rate. The banks now lend the $3000 to the private sector at 10 percent annual interest for all types of loans.

We now have $1000 of debt-free money circulating in the economy, which was spent into circulation by the national Treasury for its annual budget expenditures, and $3000 that was borrowed and spent into circulation by the private sector for its needs. The private sector pays interest at a rate of 10 percent on its loans.

At the end of the year, the private sector owes $300 in interest on its interest-bearing debt, plus the principal, or $3300. The private sector removes $3300 from the economy and pays this sum to the banks, satisfying its principal and interest payments. The banks repay the $3000 to the national Treasury plus the interest at 3 percent, or a total of $3090. The banks keep $210, the difference between the 10 percent they charged and the 3 percent they paid, as their profit on the transaction.

When the $3090 is returned to the national Treasury by the banks, the money is effectively removed from circulation. Since the Treasury is the only creative source of money, it does not need to make a profit. Whenever it needs money for a public expenditure, it simply writes a check against no funds, just as the privately owned Federal Reserve banks currently do when they lend or spend.

One can easily see from Exhibit 16 that of the $4000 that was added to the economy (EA), $3300 of this was removed by the private sector to repay its debt of $3000 at 10 percent interest. This payment leaves $700 of purchasing power in the economy. If this excess is allowed to accumulate in the economy on an annual basis, it may lead to monetary imbalance in the economic arena. It will *not* cause inflation, but it will decrease private borrowing from banks. Reduced commercial borrowing means reduced interest payments as a business expense, hence lower inflation, but it may also lead to a state that was recently described to me by a friend who deals in international barter.

My friend was exporting a steady supply of fresh fruits and vegetables from the Island of Dominica in the Caribbean to London on a daily basis. His supply was consistent for about six months, but it then became very irregular. He went to Dominica to find out the reason for this supply problem. He learned from the suppliers that each one of them needed only about $900 per year to live the life to which they were accustomed. Since they each had already earned $900, they could afford not to work or produce any fruits and vegetables until the following year. Excess purchasing power in the economy then could lead to decreased production and to a shortage of products and services. Given such a shortage, the "greed factor" would trigger inflation.

To avoid this kind of inflation from occurring, a special tax must be levied to remove close to $700 from the economy. The money would flow into the national Treasury for extinguishment. Once the $700 is removed by this special tax, the tax would have served its purpose—to maintain a balance in the monetary system. To maintain an equilibrium, there should remain in the economy at all times an excess of debt-free money against the amount of money that is removed by the private sector for payment of interest on its borrowed principal. This special tax would only be triggered when the annual government debt-free expenditures are far in excess of the interest amount being annually removed by the private sector to satisfy interest payments.

If you designate the annual government budget expenditure authorized by the government as GE, the annual private sector interest payments to banks as I, and the total amount of excess purchasing power that needs to be removed in the form of a special tax as T, then to maintain the balance in a combined debt-free and debt monetary system the formula would be:

$$GE = I + \{T \text{ (as needed)}\}$$

With this mathematical concept, the government can spend as much as 50 percent of what the private sector spends and still maintain a reasonably stable purchasing power for our money.

We have landed men on the moon and brought them back safely. We have put sophisticated probes into deep outer space to provide us with a wealth of scientific information, such as *Voyager's* incredible photographs of the planet Neptune four billion miles away, yet we are slaves to a monetary system that grew out of an ancient goldsmith banking depository system that was flawed. It is incomprehensible that the problem has not been solved before now.

We can design a monetary system that will provide a reasonably stable purchasing power for our money. After all, money is nothing more than a medium that converts our labor into units that we exchange for goods denominated in like units, that is, our labor and productivity measured by a scale of wages.

With the adoption of such a monetary system how will America fare in the international economy? Better than any other nation. With the national Treasury creating money, we will wipe out the boom and bust of economic cycles, and we will have a continuous stream of productivity and full employment. Since commercial borrowings will decrease when there is an adequate money supply in the economy there will be less interest payments passed on to the prices of goods and services. This will result in cheaper goods and services in the global market.

Also, we will be able to produce comparable products for less or superior products for the same prices. America will prosper beyond imagination. Other countries will prefer our goods and services that will be superior or cheaper, or both. And if they want to survive in the global economic arena, they too will have to put an end to the exploitation of the productive elements of their society by an all-debt monetary system. They will have to adopt the solution presented here. Thus, all countries will be infected with the virus of *prosperity*!

In addition, since this adoption will put a lid on inflation, our money will have a more stable purchasing power and will thus be sought after in the international money markets. Thus, the U.S. dollar will become the standard of international exchange.

Given that we can establish a reasonably stable purchasing power for our money, if we do not move to achieve it a disturbing question arises: "Why do we not *demand* a reasonably stable purchasing power for our money?" Are our elected representatives deliberately allowing a handful of private citizens to confiscate systematically and quasi-legally the tangible wealth from the productive elements of society? Are we in the midst of some vast conspiracy? Another disturbing question can also arise: "Will the handful of people who will eventually possess all the wealth without any effort or labor but rather through the ownership and control of our present debt-dominant monetary system want to maintain democratic elections after they control all the wealth of the American people?"

Inalienable Rights

"I do solemnly swear, that I will support and defend the Constitution of the United States against all enemies foreign and domestic; and I will bear true faith and allegiance to the same; that I take this obligation freely without any mental reservation or purpose of evasion; and that I will well and faithfully discharge the duties of the office on which I am about to enter so help me God."

This oath is taken by all officers elected or appointed to civil positions or who become members of the Armed Services of the United States. What percentage of the people who take this oath fully know and understand what is written in the United States Constitution?

On June 15, 1215, in a meadow at Runnymede, a band of oppressed and angry barons cornered King John of England and, at the point of a sword, wrung from him the most important civil document written up to that time and possibly ever after, the Magna Charta. Scholars doubt that our own Declaration of Independence and Constitution could have been written without the foundation laid by that English charter.

The keys to our very freedom are provided in the *Constitution of the United States of America*. Without a doubt, one of the most important rights we as citizens have is provided in Article 1, Section 8, Clause 5: "The Congress shall have power . . . to coin money, regulate the value thereof, and of foreign coin, and fix the standard of weights and measures."

The word "coin" means "to create." The framers of the Constitution could not have possibly meant to create only coins, since in 1787 when Article 1, Section 8 was written there was no U.S. coin of any kind, no official U.S. Treasury, and no U.S. mint. The first mint did not appear until

1792. Article 1, Section 8, Clause 5, clearly means that it is the right of Congress to create all forms of money.

Whether some insidious conspiracy exists or whether we are heir to a monumental mistake, it is only a matter of time before the deadly debt virus transfers all the wealth of the productive sector of society into the hands of the money creators. Only the large stockholders of the Federal Reserve banks will be the eventual inheritors that will also swallow up the smaller banks.

Chapter 12

Debt, Death and Destruction

Debt is a state of continuing bondage. Once engulfed by debt one knows no rest or peace of mind. Be out of debt and experience true freedom.

TOMORROW IS MOTHER'S DAY

Yesterday there stood in Potter's Field, beside an open grave, the forlorn figure of a weary man. His gray-haired head was bowed. His spare shoulders drooped as though under a heavy load, and they shuddered and convulsed with grief. Tears fell from his dark, hollow eyes upon the fresh-dug earth of Potter's Field. It is hard to watch an old man weep.

Rough, careless hands quickly lowered a cheap, wooden coffin to the bottom of the damp grave. Shovels were seized and the dreary sound of clods thumping upon the lid of the wooden box echoed softly. The lonely man moved close, peered down through the rising dust into the yawning tomb and all the tenderness and love, all the desolate sadness, all the heartbroken agony of all the world was expressed by his mournful cry of a single word. That word was "Mother."

No, she was not his mother who was being buried there, but his wife. But his term of endearment for her through the years had been "Mother." Ever since their sons were born 40 years ago he had called her "Mother." The two fine boys were the idols of their mother's heart and the pride of their father's life. But they had heard what they thought to be the call to what they mistook for duty and had been killed in battles fought on distant, foreign soil.

When the word arrived of the death of the first, and then within a month, the death of the second son, the very earth seemed to reel and rock and the foundations of the universe appeared to dissolve beneath the parents' feet.

Nothing mattered now. "Mother" moved about as in a trance, and the stunned father could scarcely pull himself together. Finally, he was told that he was too old to do the work required of him though he was only 46, and a younger man took his place. For a while, he worked at any odd job he could find, but soon there were none of these. One day he and his wife received notice the payment on the mortgage on their home was overdue and must be paid at once. In a futile effort, the man tried to find work to earn the necessary money, but he was 47 now, and who would employ a man of that advanced age?

He saw the banker and reminded him that he had paid $3,000 on the $1,500 mortgage—$1800 going for interest, $1,200 to reduce the principal and that now, after 22 years, only $300 remained unpaid. He begged for leniency. An extension of three months was granted but they proved to be months of frustration and terrible foreboding. The appointed day arrived and with it a notice from the bank to vacate within two weeks, or he would be forcibly evicted. The little mother's crushed heart was in her home. She had been brought to it as a bride. Her boys had been born there. Millions of sweet memories clung to its every board and sash and sill. The trees, the birds, the shrubs, the flowers and the smooth lawn were all intimate friends.

The old home had a sentimental value of more than a million dollars and now it must be lost for a paltry $300, originally created with a flick of a pen by a banker.

What new horrors did the future hold?—The awful uncertainty. Where could they go? What could they do? They had no money to rent another place nor to move elsewhere. Baffled, stunned, defeated, all they could do, it seemed, was wait and pray that the heart of the banker would soften.

The fateful day arrived and with it an order to vacate, and men came to see that the order was obeyed. Ruthlessly, the furniture, pictures, knickknacks, clothing and all were piled in a jumbled heap on the lawn.

The little mother was helped to a chair beneath the palm tree she had planted the spring her first baby was born. Her husband gently stroked her hair and placed a protecting arm around her shoulders—small protection indeed against the hosts of entrenched bankers' greed. A decision was made. Their belongings must be sold to supply their present need. A secondhand dealer was called and upon arriving, arrogantly asked, "Well, what do you want for this pile of junk?"

A pitifully few dollars bought those objects which were more precious than gold to those who had sacrificed through the long years to accumulate them. The lawn was soon cleared and arm in arm the two quietly trudged slowly down the familiar street as the sun sank behind the western hills.

Twenty years have passed since that man and his wife were dispossessed. For 20 years he did his best to earn an honest living and for 20 years he lived in rooms, cubbyholes, garrets, or wherever he could find shelter. She worked too, as she could—scrubbing, sewing, washing, nursing—but always with an aching heart. At 58 years of age she put down her load and died. Yesterday, she was given a Christian burial in Potter's Field. The old man will trudge on along, for tomorrow is "Mother's Day."[1]

In an all-debt monetary system, total debt is unpayable. Unpayable debt frequently leads directly to death and destruction. The collapse of civilizations in ancient Egypt, ancient Babylon, ancient Persia, ancient Greece, and the Roman Empire were all directly related to a debt-dominant monetary system that allowed for the automatic transfer of the tangible wealth from the productive elements of civilization to the money creators. With the collapse of each civilization, the death toll was enormous.

Five hundred thousand children died in 1988 because developing countries slashed their social welfare programs to pay the staggering amount of interest due to foreign and American commercial banks. These deaths were reported by the United Nations Children's Fund.

In May 1989, the mayor of Houston was interviewed on public radio about a new city drive to feed the many thousands of hungry men, women, and children in the city. Questioned about why such a drive was necessary, the mayor responded that the city did not have enough money to provide food and shelter for the unemployed and hungry. Imagine hunger and starvation in the richest country on this planet, all due to a shortage of money—money that has no intrinsic value and needs no special raw materials or backing for its creation! In my years of research, I have met no more than a handful of people who truly have some understanding of the science of money. I find it puzzling, no, incomprehensible, that the most commonly used of all the creations of man—money—is the least understood.

World Crisis

It is quite obvious that an all-debt monetary system will ultimately ruin any nation and every person in the nation except the money creator and lender. Simple history reveals that fact. Aristotle articulated the truth about money three hundred years before the birth of Christ when he observed that money cannot procreate.

Andrae Nordskog in his splendid book, *We Bankers*, relates a rather startling incident that graphically illustrates that we cannot keep going in the direction in which we are headed without confronting disaster. He states:

In February, 1850, our State of California issued bonds in the sum of $934.40 to pay for a granite slab to be placed at the 120-foot level inside of Washington's Monument on the grounds of our nation's capitol. On the slab is the following inscription: "California, youngest of the union, brings her golden tribute to the memory of its father." Our Golden State issued short-term bonds bearing interest at the rate of 36 percent annually. In 1873, new bonds in the amount of $2,277,500.00 were issued to retire the original bonds. Between that time and 1941 the state has paid over $10 million in interest but not one cent on the principal.[2]

For whom is democracy working? We are not flirting with economic disaster—the courtship is already over and we are entrenched in a perilous relationship.

During the first week of March 1989, about one thousand people died and more than two thousand were injured in Venezuelan riots and looting, sparked by the further tightening of the bankers'-dictated austerity screws. Rising bus fares and the price of gasoline by 89 percent and, in the same week, the price of bread by 100 percent, broke the camel's back and drove the enraged poor into the streets to loot and carry off anything that could be carried or carted away.

The people did not loot or riot for their own entertainment. They looted because that was the only way they could get food, clothing, or furniture. People without jobs, hungry, with undernourished children, without clothing and adequate shelter are not likely to lie down and play dead. They may be poor and docile, but they are not stupid. They see the abundance of food, clothing, and fine homes. They understand that the only thing between them and their dreams is a job and some money.

Perhaps they'll discover that it is the foreign bankers parading as benefactors who have ensnared their government in debt and are to blame for their woes. Maybe then they will throw out the central bankers and the foreign bankers and ask their own government treasuries to create their money interest-free. If so, the banker-imposed shackles of poverty in the midst of plenty will be broken.

The major stumbling block in the way of prosperity and plenty is a medium of exchange that can be created simply by the stroke of a pen or a computer entry. Yet there is runaway inflation, poverty, and abuse. Third world countries are clamoring for economic relief, but as long as their sovereign governments are permitting their nation's money supply to be created as debt by national and international commercial bankers, they have no way to extricate themselves from their debt-shackles.

Every bank loan and every bank rescheduling plan further tightens the debt and deficit screws. Will the money creators get a full stranglehold on these governments and deceptively foreclose on the wealth and assets of those nations?

Latin American external debt is increasing exponentially. Argentina has a debt of more than $56 billion. Brazil has a debt of more than $140 billion, and Chile owes more than $20 billion. The debt in Mexico has swollen to $100 billion, debt in Peru is $16 billion, and Venezuelan debt is more than $30 billion. At the close of 1988, the regional debt for the Latin American countries was more than $420 billion, and the loans that produced this debt were all made with checkbook money.

Brazil pays about $30 million of interest per day in foreign exchange funds. This money would build about six hundred homes per day valued at $50,000 each or over two hundred thousand homes per year. This amount is the "real value" the bankers force the Brazilian government to channel into the pockets of private bankers through these austerity programs.

The entire planet is suffering from a debt crisis, including Canada, Europe—particularly Eastern Europe—Asia, Australia, New Zealand, Russia, and Japan. Although Japan, West Germany, Taiwan, Korea, and Hong Kong seem to be doing well economically, it is only a matter of time before their debt starts to increase exponentially. They, too, will have their turn as the victim of a debt-dominant monetary system.

Guyana

On a recent trip to Guyana, my place of birth, this problem took on a personal countenance. This small country, located on the northern coast of South America, has reached its national debt limit. The variables that determine national debt limits are as numerous as the indebted countries themselves; however, nations that have surpassed debt boundaries have at least one thing in common—an impoverished standard of living.

Unemployment is rampant in this country, with more than 35 percent of the population out of work. Men, women, and children can be seen begging for money to provide life's barest necessities; many people have never experienced a day's work. If employed, however, the average Guyanese earns between G$30 and G$45 per day, the equivalent of 60 to 90 cents in U.S. dollars. The inflationary economy makes most purchases prohibitive—lunch for two at an average restaurant may cost as much as G$1,000; a new car demands G$1.5 million (a subcompact at that).

Housing is stark with few of the amenities that we Americans deem necessary. Small, clapboard houses, most in disrepair, line the narrow streets. There is sporadic indoor plumbing, but electricity is available—sometimes. Hot water is unavailable even to the wealthiest citizen, and air conditioning is almost unheard of in this tropical climate.

Grocery stores require very few decisions. Many ordinary items cannot be obtained, and the "well-stocked" department stores display bare shelves. This reality encourages a sound black market to fill in the product gaps.

The quality of health care is poor, and the infant mortality rate is a painfully high 20 percent. The local hospital inspires no confidence in either the quality of its care or its sanitation practices. Childhood illnesses that are no longer considered a problem in this country still wreak havoc on Guyanese children.

Public and private transportation is crude. Aged and unreliable automobiles litter the many unpaved streets. Those that are able to own a car, despite the exorbitant price tag, are often hindered by the lack of a constant supply of gasoline and replacement parts.

Though the topography and climate are conducive to bauxite mining and rice, cotton, and sugar cane cultivation, the country has been so debilitated by its debt situation that trade has become counterproductive. The Guyanese dollar has no influence on international markets, making matters even worse. Production is at a morbid standstill. A mere thirty years ago, Guyana was the breadbasket of the Caribbean.

The human toll is high. Eighty-five percent of the citizens of Guyana are literate; but, unlike the United States where education usually offers a greater freedom of opportunity, here it only makes the limited choices more obvious. The desperate economic situation has forced some to choose escape over commitment—many of the better-educated Guyanese youth leave the country in pursuit of a higher standard of living and a more hopeful future.

The government appears paralyzed by the situation. Public officials are forced to abide by International Monetary Fund mandates in exchange for much-needed loans from the privately owned World Bank. These very mandates, however, have forced the rapid and frequent devaluation of the Guyanese dollar, which continues to feather the nests of the rich while taking money from the pockets of the poor.

What happened to this country that was once considered the garden spot of the Caribbean? Its external debt of $1.2 billion, or $60 billion Guyanese, proved to be more than this small country could support. It is impossible to carry a large debt burden while maintaining a healthy, growing economy that fosters the well-being of its constituency. The message is deafening, but apparently the lesson is yet to be learned.

The United States

The United States is the greatest debtor nation in the world. Our public debt is well over $3 trillion and escalating exponentially as of February 1991. Our president and his economic advisers keep telling us that all is economically well in the United States. I know better, and hopefully by now you do, too.

The central bankers and finance ministers of the world met in Berlin in September of 1988 at the annual gathering of the World Bank and the International Monetary Fund (IMF). They were confronted by the grim evidence of their power. That evidence was a global economy largely driven by the need to keep up with IOUs.

Decades of debt financing and six years of the debt crisis have deepened the chasm between the rich and poor nations, warned a report prepared for the conference under the direction of Dr. Karl Holzapfel, a noted German economist. "The advanced societies of the West produce goods and services; the Third World just produces debt," concluded the survey. (The Third World may produce debt, but it is the private bankers who *create* debt solely for their own benefit.) "Leading industrial nations should not take comfort from their favored position," cautioned Holzapfel. "The United States in particular, teeters perilously on the edge of the debt pit that has swallowed up so many lesser economies," said the survey.[3]

Faced with such ominous facts from every side, even free trade establishment economists such as Paul McCracken privately talk about the coming "worldwide economic disintegration," said policy consultant Dr. Paul Adler, a participant at the IMF conference.[4] Shackled by debt and mired in stagflation, economies of less developed countries are deteriorating very rapidly. The following developments were cited at the conference. Black African countries, among the poorest anywhere, now collectively owe just about twice as much—some $230 billion—as at the start of the debt crisis, which most economists date from August 1982. In a typical African nation, Adler picked Mali as an example, the IOUs due to international banks, $1.4 billion, surpassed the yearly total output of goods and services. During the six years of the crisis, all international bank debt rose by some 40 percent. Despite desperate efforts to retire some of their debt by means of forced sale of land or other assets, both Brazil and Mexico were unable to bring down their debts one penny.

Anyone who thinks the contagion of terminal debt fever will not spread from Mexico, Argentina, Brazil, and Mali to the United States need only take a look at this nation's floundering savings and loan industry. The collapse of the thrifts and related financial disasters saddled the American taxpayer with a monstrous bail-out bill of well over $600 billion. What a travesty of justice!

President Bush has proposed legislation to reform our banking system. The proposed reforms will broaden the services banks provide so that they can compete with other institutions like mortgage banks, insurance companies, and brokerage houses. In addition, the banks will be allowed to have interstate branch banking. Such reforms will only lead to consolidation of the banking industry. The smaller banks will be eliminated, and thus competition will be greatly decreased. However, such reforms to solve our banking crisis, are only grasping at straws, when in fact, the reformers do not understand what the crisis is all about. The commercial banking industry crisis is just around the corner and will suffer the same devastating plight of the current Savings and Loans. The only difference is that the coming commercial banking system failure will make the Savings and Loan crisis look like a Sunday afternoon picnic. And, who do you think will be forced to pay the tab for the multi-trillion dollar bail out? Yes, you guessed it, you and I, the American taxpayers. Are we accomplices to the enslavement of our children? Yes, unless we take immediate action against the money creators.

Banks create money out of thin air solely for their own benefit, not understanding that the all-debt money system is a double-edged sword that will also decimate many banks and cause their demise. The unsuspecting taxpayer is burdened with the despicable task of resuscitating the failing banks. There can be no greater form of injustice in a democracy. This is surely a heinous crime against the American taxpayer.

Daily headlines afford more evidence of the fateful combination of forces working in our economy. Michael Milken, the so-called "junk-bond" king, made his fortune by swapping equity for debt and took advantage of the corporate tax laws to fund that land shark, the corporate raider. Do you remember when RJR Nabisco became a takeover target and that company's high-quality, AAA debt became "junk"?

Nor is the "pure" equity holder immune from the ravages of our flawed monetary system. Warren Buffett, possibly the preeminent investor in America, sounded an alarm in the late 1970s when he wrote an article for *Fortune* magazine. In it he explained how inflation "robs the equity investor." Buffett wisely likened ownership of dividend-paying stock to a perpetual coupon bond, indexed to inflation. He had a finger on the problem but did not fully articulate what it was.[5]

There is a way out of these quasi-legal debt shackles for all debtor nations if the leaders of the people will *acquire the knowledge and courage* to dislodge the bankers' money monopolies in their nations. The first step is for central banks in all these countries to be dissolved and made a part of their respective national treasuries. The collective goal must be to return the money creation process to the people, and change it to a balanced monetary system.

The governments, through their treasuries, should take over the money creation process and finance their own economies, eliminating austerity programs. They should outlaw the creation of money by private corporations and individuals. The government treasuries should take over all their nations' check-clearing operations, thus putting an end to the fractional reserve practice of commercial bankers. When these debtor governments operate through their national treasuries, creating debt-free money for public expenditures and debt-money loans through the banking system for private enterprise, they will supply their economies with all the funds needed to put their labor forces to work and produce tangible wealth. Of course, the government will have to be the sole clearinghouse for checks and have the ability to tax the excess purchasing power out of the economy.

Given this scenario, the world will see the birth of a new era, where economies deal in abundance instead of scarcity, where hunger, disease, illiteracy, and poverty are wiped out.

Chapter 13

Vaccine for the Debt Virus

Usury is a cancer which plagues commerce and breeds rampant greed; a malady which is cured with surgical swiftness through logic and wisdom.

Conventional economic dicta have not provided answers to problems in the United States or in other countries faced with unemployment, inflation, currency devaluation, and the myriad of other manifestations of a debt-based monetary system. The monetization of debt—the way money is created in the United States and in other nations—is a problem that has never been adequately addressed by conventional economic wisdom.

There is a deep-seated psychological need within most of us to seek certainty in areas where no certainty is possible, and economics has pretended to assume that role. Economics does not work, though, when its practitioners do not identify cause and effect relationships and the consequences thereof.

190

It is not possible to adequately address economics without considering these two facts: debt is central to the money creation process, and debt carries an interest charge. Most economists readily agree that money is created as debt, but they stop there and virtually ignore the consequences of the interest charge. One cannot conduct a study of anatomy and physiology without considering the body as a whole. The body currently under examination by mainstream economists has vital organs missing. *Any economist who does not fully understand the anatomy and physiology of money will be no better than a general surgeon who has little or no knowledge of human anatomy and physiology.*

The demand for answers to the problems that confront our society will always outweigh the answers supplied because so few people are original thinkers. Most of us accept as gospel what appears in print—often written by individuals with sufficient years of practice as economists to have made one or two good "calls" about what the future holds.

In reality, the accuracy of the majority of predictions made by economists is near zero. Financially, the world will be a far better place when scientists examine cause and effect relationships and use these relationships as the linchpin of their work rather than sociopolitical mumbo jumbo legitimized by numerology. If this sounds harsh, it is because I demand excellent results in my work. Conventional economic theory provides results of the narrowest magnitude.

Money in and of itself has no intrinsic value. It should be a measure of productive effort, it should serve as a medium of exchange and a store of value, it should facilitate the transfer of goods and services, and it should be difficult to counterfeit, among other desirable attributes. Understanding what money is will clarify our understanding of the economy. We work in order to trade our labor output for the output of other workers; money is not, contrary to common belief, the object of work.

Money should be treated as a public utility. When it is created, it should belong to the sovereign authority of a country—that is, to the national treasury and the government of that country. H. L. Hunt, the late American oilman, summed up the real use of money when he said, "Money only makes accounting convenient."

A Plan of Action

I have spent considerable time focusing on the flaws of the all-debt monetary system. If there is an illness, hopefully a treatment exists for that illness. If no treatment exists and the illness is of sufficient consequence, however, researchers should work diligently to develop one.

The problems created by the all-debt monetary system demand a frontal attack. Central banks not owned by governments should be dissolved, and private banks will then be under a 100 percent reserve requirement. Banks thus chartered and organized ought to be lending only what they have or what they can borrow; they must not be creating money.

Essential laws must be passed to de-politicize the monetary process. These laws would ensure that government is not in the business of banking, and that the banks do not function like the Treasury should function—creating and providing the national government and the economy with the primary supply of money. Under a sensible debt-free monetary system, it is legally the government's business, through its national Treasury, to print, create, and provide coins, paper, or checkbook money for the national economy.

Silently allowing banks to create their own money—to monetize debt as currently practiced—gives banks and bank-associated businesses and investment purveyors definite financial advantages over all other segments of the so-called free enterprise system. The present system elevates the banking industry to a financial aristocracy, allowing unconstitutional control over the money creation process when, in fact, this process ought to be under the absolute dominion of government. Remember, we do not work for money—we work so that our labor (our production) might be exchanged for the labor of others (their production). Money just provides the accounting for this exchange.

Getting something for nothing violates fundamental moral and physical laws. Banks can now create billions of dollars of checkbook money, which they lend, spend, or invest with ease. The interest earned on a billion dollars is one thousand times greater than that earned on $1 million, all other things being equal. Money should serve all players equally in the economic arena. We must think of it as nothing more than a public utility, and as such, it should be created for the good of all. Does the present system serve the good of all?

Remember, we work so that we may exchange our labor (our production) for the labor of others (their labor). Money is a means whereby the exchange process is made easier. This is worth repeating because our thinking goes awry when we merge this fundamental, concrete fact with prevailing economic theory. "Money is not, properly speaking, one of the subjects of commerce," David Hume wrote in 1758, "but only the instrument which men have agreed upon to facilitate the exchange of one commodity for another. It is none of the wheels of trade; it is the oil which renders the motion of the wheels more smooth and easy."

It would be cumbersome and chaotic for each citizen of a country to create his own money, so in a democratic country, the national treasury should create all money and clear all checks. The banking industry should operate as a private enterprise serving as an intermediary between the national treasury and producers and consumers operating in the private sector.

Under this system, it is important that the national Treasury clear all checks. If the clearing process is not controlled, private banks could continue to practice their archaic fractional reserve deposit expansion money system and no one would be the wiser. In addition, the banking system should be required to operate with a 100 percent reserve as Dr. Milton Friedman proposed in 1954. This would forestall any "runs" on banks.

The essence of popular argument against allowing government to create money goes something like this: "Put the money creation process in the hands of the politicians? You can't trust those damn crooks. They will print too much money and there will be runaway inflation." I say, "Hogwash." There is no mathematical relationship between the quantity of money and the prices of goods and services. One can quantify prices with regards to production and services and total expenditures, but it is impossible to quantify greed. There are three things that are the ultimate causes of price inflation. One is the interest payments to banks on commercial loans, another is greed—the basic, human foible of wanting something for nothing—and a legal devaluation of money.

Legislation

The government must enact laws with regards to the creation and control of money and credits. Money and credits should be controlled by laws and not policies since policy can be changed on whim. Laws, on the other hand, cannot be changed without due legislative process.

The supply of money should meet its demand in the marketplace. Government bonds would no longer be issued to create money or credits. They would not be necessary because money needs no backing. If you try to back money, then the quantity of money in the marketplace would be limited by the availability of the backing. If the backing is not available and the quantity of money in the marketplace needs to be increased because of increased demand, then the quantity of money could not be increased at a time when it is most needed. Remember that money is simply a means whereby the productivity of the work force is accounted for. As productivity increases, the means of facilitating the exchange of goods and services must correspondingly grow to allow the process to continue.

Under this system, income taxes and most other taxes will be abolished. If government is creating money for public expenditures, there is no need to tax the citizens to finance those expenditures or to provide monies to pay the interest charge on public debt, because there is no public debt. To control inflation and have a stable monetary unit, the national Treasury should give interest-free or low-interest loans for any needed, achievable, approved, and worthy projects that would benefit the country as a whole and that have legislative authorization.

The national treasury would create money and purchase interest-bearing bonds from the borrowing banks. The interest rate charged on all treasury loans would be determined by the treasury's computer, which could be programmed to maintain the flow of treasury revenues in close balance with the flow of treasury expenditures.

Under this balanced system, banks would operate just like savings and loans used to operate prior to the reforms adopted in 1980 under the Banking Deregulation Act. They could lend out of the pool of their savers' deposits; they could also borrow from the treasury and lend this money to their customers. The important factor in this system is that the supply of money would invariably meet the demand for it, and the system would remain in balance.

Debt-free government expenditures should be in balance with interest payments to banks. Under such a system, the economy expands or contracts on the basis of how willing and able the citizens are to produce and consume, not on how willing or able the monetary authority is to create money. The treasury must be the one and only source of new money.

Money would be added to the economy through debt-free government expenditures and through loans made by the treasury mainly to banks or, in certain cases, directly to industry. Under this system, banks would be just like any other business enterprise. They would not create money, nor would they receive any free raw material like reserves. The principal source of their lendable funds would be the savings of the people. If banks did need more money, they could borrow from the national treasury. Bank profits would be derived from their ability to offer fee paid services and to lend profitably from the savings of depositors or from their own or borrowed funds in competition with other banks.

Authorized national government expenditures would be paid for with checks written by the national Treasury against no funds—just like the privately owned Federal Reserve banks do at the present time. These checks will pay for public needs such as national defense, schools, public highways, the post office, space program, entitlements, and so on. Money would flow back to the treasury as principal and interest payments on loans to the private sector, including banks, but not through the Internal Revenue Service, *which should be dissolved.*

Mankind seems content to become slave to rules once they are promulgated. We seem to forget that we make the rules, and that they exist so that we can have a better and more comfortable life. When rules no longer accomplish their purposes, it is time we abolish them and move on to others that will better serve the needs of the many and not the desires of the few.

Any Objections?

A government creating money—doesn't this sound like communism? But, if the communist countries are creating debt-free money to finance their public expenditures, then why do they have so much debt—the Communist bloc owes billions of dollars to Western banks—and poverty?

No, money created by the government is not a trait of communism. Communism is crumbling today not because those governments were creating money but because those governments did not understand the functions of money in a free society. More importantly, they did not understand the proper management of money, nor did they understand the meaning of "incentive." Communism took away the incentive for people to produce.

The national Treasury is the soundest system to preserve and promote the best interests of a truly free enterprise economy. Today, there is no country on this planet with a truly free enterprise economy, and as long as money is created and controlled by a handful in the private sector, there never can be.

In a balanced monetary system, the government creates money in response to the needs of the people. If the government needs to spend money, the expenditures will be spent debt-free for the good of all the citizens, not just a handful of them.

Under the present system, the money creation process benefits only a handful—the present money creators. These include the Federal Reserve, commercial banks, and thrift institutions. Of these, only the Federal Reserve banks are immune to failure. They can write limitless checks against no funds because they clear their own checks and do not possess an account at some other bank. The ability of commercial banks and the thrift institutions to create new money is limited by their reserve requirements, which are set by the Federal Reserve banks. When a national government creates money, though, the balance between its creation and its extinguishment will be governed by mathematical law. Money should not be created according to policy as in the United States today, but by law.

There is a great difference between policy and law. Policy is changeable; policy decisions can drastically reduce the amount of credit available in the economic arena, and such reductions can precipitate a serious economic depression. Policy decisions can also encourage or discourage lending to a particular sector of the economy and thus lead to prosperity or failure respectively in that sector.

Monetary policy can be arbitrary or even dangerous to the health of an economy, but a monetary system linked to mathematical law that is impartial and unemotional will be fair to all citizens. In a balanced monetary system operated by a national government, monetary authority can be locked into law and arbitrary policy decisions can be permanently obliterated. In such a system, the amount of money in the system can vary according to demand alone. Interest rates can be set scientifically, operating without emotion and outside policy decisions, and so can remain stable. All worthy, needed, and achievable public and private sector enterprises can have the opportunity to move ahead without being hindered by a shortage in the supply of money in the economy.

Economic conditions the world over are deteriorating. Communism is falling apart. Communist bloc countries are trying to embrace a free democracy, and several states within Russia are seceding. These are only some of the unmistakable signs that the all-debt money system practiced by the whole planet, with the exception of the Channel Islands, is bankrupt. Economic "geniuses" all over the world are attempting to solve the economic woes of debt-ridden Third World countries by instituting austerity programs such as currency devaluations and increased taxes, only with disastrous results—especially for the productive elements of society.

The present all-debt money system, with its inherent mathematical impossibilities, seems to produce irrational behavior by governments. The public, consequently, tends to discredit government officials and to doubt the democratic process. Government must learn to function efficiently or face an enraged electorate.

Politicians should wake up to the fact that they have the ultimate legislative power to govern effectively and control money creation. When this truth is accepted and embraced, more citizens will begin to understand that they are working not to "make" money but to create wealth by the sweat of their brow.

There are numerous advantages to governments when the national treasury is the only source of money creation and check-clearing.

- Money will be available in adequate amounts at all times, at low interest rates.
- Business activity will be continuous, and employment will be available for those willing and able to work.

- Economic growth will only be limited by our imagination.
- Inflation will never be reduced to zero as long as mankind suffers greed, but its march will be severely hampered, thus protecting wages and savings.
- Bankruptcies, foreclosures, business failures, and unemployment will no longer be tools used to balance prosperity.
- It will no longer be impossible to repay the total private debt.
- Prices will diminish along with debt and stabilize when debt is payable.
- Boom and bust cycles will permanently disappear.
- All debt held at the current time, both by the public and private sector, will fall and reach a level below that of the money supply.
- Interest will no longer grow into an ever-increasing, unpayable debt.
- Government borrowing will cease because it will no longer be necessary; taxation will drastically decline, and government can phase out the Internal Revenue Service.
- Public debt can be reduced to zero, with governments earning interest on account balances rather than paying interest on debt.
- All working people will be able to afford homes and cars and can save to enjoy comfortable and dignified retirement without depending on handouts from the government.
- Usury will be abolished; the banking industry will be like any other business in a truly free enterprise system, practicing competitive banking.

Key Elements of the "Cure"

To summarize: The national Treasury will be the sole source of original money issue.

- All existing laws and codes allowing money creation by private banks will be repealed.
- The national Treasury will be the sole clearing house for all checks.
- The government will enact a law that the national Treasury will coin, create, provide, and regulate money and money credits for all the requirements of the nation, both public and private. All money needed to meet national government obligations will be debt-free.
- The national Treasury will service the money needs of the private sector through loans to banks and other private entities.
- The interest rate charged by the national Treasury on all loans to the private sector will be regulated mathematically so that money will be withdrawn from circulation at a rate that will maintain a balance with Treasury expenditures.
- Private banks, institutions, and individuals will be prohibited from creating money.
- State and local government treasuries will receive interest-free loans from the national Treasury to finance local, voter-approved projects.
- All legitimate financial obligations of the national Treasury in effect when the balanced monetary system law is enacted will remain in force until paid.
- Government borrowing will cease, because it becomes unnecessary.

Chapter 14

Midas Touch or Fraud and Usury?

*Written laws are like spiders' webs and will, like them,
only entangle and hold the poor and weak while the rich and
powerful easily break through them.*
                    Anacharcis, Scythian philosopher, 600 B.C.

As a youngster, I rode an Italian passenger ship from
British Guyana, my native country, to Southampton, England. I vividly remember looking up at the large, gray structures with names like Barclays Bank, Lloyds Bank, and
Westminster Bank as I walked through the streets of London. These buildings conveyed a richness I had not dreamed
of or imagined. They were peopled with aloof individuals
who were absolute wizards in money matters, or so I thought.
In those days, almost 30 years ago, my only real thought of
money and banks was that I did not have any money, so I
had no real business in a bank.

A decade later, after achieving a medical degree, I came
to the United States for postgraduate training in surgery.

Years later, after establishing my private practice in Humble, Texas, I was appointed to the board of directors of a local bank. From this experience I came to conclude that banking did not fit my previous notions of lofty stature. I discovered that bankers were quite ordinary people with varied backgrounds and different levels of abilities. Many had no college training, and those who did frequently had a degree totally unrelated to finance, banking, or money. Many were frankly dishonest; they would not hesitate to lie under oath.

I arranged to speak with Stephen K. Huber, professor of law at the University of Houston, to collect data for this chapter. Professor Huber is an acknowledged authority on banking laws and regulations. He explained to me that law is the collective organization of the rights of individuals to lawful defense. Each of us has a natural right to defend his person, his liberty, and his property. These are our most basic rights. The preservation of any one of these three, however, is dependent upon the preservation of the other two.

Our faculties are but extensions of our individuality. And our properties are but extensions of our faculties. If every person has a right to defend his person, his liberty, and his property, then it follows that a group of people have a right to organize and support a common force to protect these rights. The principle of collective right, its reason for existing, and its lawfulness, is thus based on the rights of the individual. The common force that protects this collective right cannot logically have any other purpose or any other mission than that for which it acts as a substitute.

Since one individual cannot lawfully use force against the person, liberty, or property of any other individual, then the common force cannot, for the same reason, lawfully be used to damage the person, liberty, or property of others, individuals, or groups. Such a perversion of force would be, in both cases, contrary to my premise.

Law today often does not confine itself to its proper function. When it has exceeded its proper function, it has not done so merely in some minor and debatable matter. Often the law has acted in a direction opposite its own purpose and has been used to destroy its own objective. Often the law has been applied to destroy the justice it was supposed to maintain and used to limit and abridge the very rights it was designed to protect. For instance, the law is being abused when it is used to take property from an individual without consent or fair compensation, and gives it to another to whom it does not belong. Laws on taxation comprise such abuses. And, this is only one example.

At times, the law has placed the collective force at the disposal of certain unscrupulous persons who wish, without risk, to exploit the person, liberty, and property of others. In some instances, law has been perverted by the influence of two entirely different forces—greed and false philanthropy.

Self-preservation and self-development are common aspirations among all peoples. If everyone could enjoy the unrestricted use of their faculties and the free disposition of the fruits of their labor, social progress would be ceaseless, uninterrupted, and fulfilling. Unfortunately, some people attempt to live and prosper at the expense of others. This observation is not rash, nor does it come from a gloomy and uncharitable spirit—the annals of history bear witness to the truth of it. Wars, mass population dislocations, religious persecutions, slavery, dishonesty in commerce, and monopolies in business are but a few examples of this human failing. This human foible has its origin in the nature of man, in that primitive and universal instinct that drives him to satisfy his desires with the least possible pain.

Man can live and satisfy his desires only by ceaseless labor; that is, by applying his skills toward the manipulation of natural resources. Through this process has come the origin of property. It is also true that man can live and satisfy his desires by seizing and consuming the products of another's labor. Without fair exchange, this process gives rise to plunder.

Now, since man is naturally inclined to avoid pain, and since labor causes a certain amount of pain, it follows that some men will resort to plunder whenever it is easier or more successful than work. Neither religion nor morality will stop it.

Professor Huber states, "The highest law of the land is the Constitution of the United States." The general misconception is that any statute passed by legislators bearing the appearance of law constitutes the law of the land. The United States Constitution is the supreme law of the land, and any statute must be in agreement with it to be valid. It is impossible for both the Constitution and a law violating it to be valid; one must prevail over the other.

The *Sixteenth American Jurisprudence*, (2nd ed., Section 256), states:

The general rule is that an unconstitutional statute, though having the form and name of law, is in reality no law, but is wholly void and ineffective for any purpose; since unconstitutionality dates from the time of its enactment and not merely from the date of the decision so branding it.

A void act cannot be legally consistent with a valid one. An unconstitutional law cannot operate to supersede any existing valid law. Indeed, insofar as a statute runs counter to the fundamental law of the land, it is superseded thereby.

Responding to questions about the nature of legal money, Professor Huber said, "Lawful money or legal tender in the United States today is Federal Reserve notes and coins, and only the U.S. government has lawful authority to create money." According to Professor Huber, "Bank charters do not provide for private commercial banks to create lawful money or legal tender. If they did, such laws would be contrary to Article 1, Section 8, Clause 5 of the U.S. Constitution which states that Congress shall have power 'to coin money and regulate the value thereof.' "

Since this section of the Constitution has never been amended and the Constitution is still the highest law in the land, according to Professor Huber, any charter granting privately owned commercial banks the right to create money would be in direct violation of the U.S. Constitution and *therefore void.*

When questioned about the legal principle *ultra vires*, Huber stated that acts *ultra vires* are acts that are in excess of the powers granted by the authority of law, or acts that are prohibited. When a corporation has no power to act but acts anyway, such actions are without legal authority. Such acts are *ultra vires.* This book has clearly established how privately owned commercial banks are creating checkbook money without the legal power to do so. The modern banking system issues receipts or IOUs for legal tender—Federal Reserve notes and coins—when it makes loans.

Bankers who are entrusted with the safekeeping of the public's money know, or should know, that the quantity of Federal Reserve notes amounts to only about 4 percent of the total money supply, and that, of the receipts for Federal Reserve notes that are issued by the banking system, 96 percent cannot be redeemed for Federal Reserve notes.

The banks should know that the receipts given in the form of checks, checkbook money, and demand deposits are for legal tender or lawful money that does not exist. Yet the loan contract that calls for repayment in lawful money implies, albeit fraudulently, that the loan has been made in lawful money. Bankers are playing the odds that no more than 10 percent of individuals who are issued receipts for lawful money will ever come into the banks to demand and claim lawful money—Federal Reserve notes.

If, however, more than the expected number of people with receipts for lawful money should show up at the doors of the bank and demand their lawful money, the bank would not be able to redeem the receipts and would be forced to shut its doors. Such an event would be described as a "run on the bank." When the bank fails, it turns to the national government for a bail out with taxpayers' money. This is grossly unfair to the American taxpayer.

The Credit Issue

Credit is the ability to borrow lawful money to obtain goods as a result of the favorable opinion held by a particular lender about our solvency and reliability. Credit also includes allowing time for making complete payment for goods. When the seller extends credit, he is not only the lender, he is also the owner of the goods. He is performing three functions: one as seller of the product, one as lender— basically lending you the money he has already expended on the product and allowing you to pay over a period of time— and one as owner of the product.

But what about bank credit? Black's Law Dictionary, 5th edition, describes "bank credit" as follows: "Money the bank owes or will lend an individual or person." It is quite clear from this definition that "bank credit" is money the bank owes or lends.

The term "credit," "checkbook money," and "demand deposits" are used synonymously by banks and refer to the money banks create whenever they make loans or investments. In other words, the term "credit" as used by a bank is its liability—something it owes. When a bank extends credit, it is not selling you a product but is lending you bank-created checkbook money that is not backed by lawful money—Federal Reserve notes. Bank credit is thus not the same type of credit as what a vendor extends.

The Bank Loan

Suppose a farmer goes to his bank to borrow $10,000 for some new machinery so he can increase production on his wheat farm. He owns his land. From the loan application, the banker sees that there is plenty of collateral in the form of tangible goods that can be sold to pay off the loan should the farmer fail to repay his loan. The loan is approved. The farmer is handed an agreement—a note saying that the farmer will repay the loan in lawful money, plus interest, over a specified period of time. If you were to ask the farmer what he borrowed, he would say he borrowed real money. But was it lawful money?

The farmer was not handed $10,000 in currency. His checking account at the bank was credited with $10,000, a simple bookkeeping entry. These numbers were not transferred from any other account at the bank, the note was "monetized" by the new demand deposits that were created by the credit to his account. What was actually loaned was a receipt for Federal Reserve notes. These receipts are only a promise to pay—not an actual payment.

The farmer has $10,000 in his checking account (the bookkeeping entry), and he writes the machinery salesman a check for $10,000. The machinery company deposits the check in its bank, and the canceled check goes to the privately owned regional Federal Reserve bank, where each commercial bank has a "reserve account." The regional commercial banks have not opened these accounts by depositing actual cash; the accounts are created as free gifts to the owners of the Federal Reserve banks—the regional commercial banks—who are members of the Federal Reserve banks.

In this transaction, lawful money was not transferred to the farmer or to the machinery salesman. What was exchanged were only "promises to pay" in Federal Reserve notes. When Bank A receives a "promise to pay" from Bank B in the form of a deposit check issued to a third party, Bank A honors that check knowing full well that its "promise to pay" will one day end up in Bank B. Banks thus exchange these "promises to pay" with each other. Professor Huber states, "A promise to pay is not actual payment."

Why does a check—a promise to pay—function as money? As long as the recipient of the check has confidence and believes the check is backed by lawful money, it is accepted. The public does not know that the checks issued by banks when they make loans are not backed by Federal Reserve notes (lawful money), and, since the private banks are the ones clearing their own checks, the public never discovers the truth—those bank checks are written against insufficient or no funds. It is illegal for you and me to write checks against insufficient or no funds. We could be prosecuted for doing what banks surreptitiously do on a daily basis. Banks have no more lawful authority to do this than we do.

Can bad checks pass as money when issued by banks? Of course they can. As long as the public does not know the checks are not backed by lawful money and as long as it has confidence that the checks are good, bad checks issued by banks as loans will pass as good money. Checks that are not backed by lawful money can pass as good money in the same manner as a counterfeit Federal Reserve note can pass as good money, if no one recognizes it as a counterfeit. The latter, however, ceases to have any value as money once it is recognized as being counterfeit. The manufacturer is called a "counterfeiter" and becomes liable to the state for commiting a crime.

Likewise, when one gets a loan from a bank in the form of a check representing the checkbook money the bank created, such a transaction should also be considered fraudulent. The person has gone to the bank to borrow lawful money, and instead the bank has created and lent only a promise to pay lawful money. Without disclosing this fact to the customer, a deliberate fraud has been perpetrated.

Not only has fraud occurred, but a breach of contract has been committed. When you sign bank papers that say you are borrowing lawful money, but the bank in reality gives privately created bank money, it is committing a breach of contract. When banks make loans, they are creating checkbook money—bookkeeping entries—with the intended purpose of circulating the same as lawful money or Federal Reserve notes and coins. Cases decided in courts of record have resulted in the following decisions:

When a contract is once declared *ultra vires*, the fact that it is executed does not validate it, nor can it be ratified so as to make it the basis of suit or action.[1]

An act is *ultra vires* when a corporation is without authority to perform it under any circumstances or for any purpose. By the doctrine of *ultra vires*, a contract made by a corporation beyond the scope of its corporate powers is unlawful.[2]

• A national bank . . . cannot lend its credit to another by becoming surety, endorser or guarantor for him, such an act is *ultra vires*.[3]

- A bank can lend its money, but not its credit.[4]
- A bank may not lend its credit to another, even though such a transaction turns out to have been of benefit to the bank.[5]

Neither is it a part of a bank's business to lend its credit. If a bank could lend its credit as well as its money, it might, if it received compensation and was careful to put its name only to solid paper, make much more than its lawful interest. Such power could create panics. Indeed, lending credit is the exact opposite of lending money, which is the real business of a bank. The latter creates a liability in favor of the bank; the former gives rise to a liability of the bank to another.[6]

We now know that, when we take out a loan at a bank, we rarely receive lawful money unless we receive cash. Yet the loan contract demands repayment of principal and interest in lawful money. If one repays the loan in lawful money when lawful money was never loaned, what is the result? Suppose you lend $100 in lawful money for one year and, at the end of the year, demand $110 back in lawful money. In effect you have charged an annual percentage rate of 10 percent.

In the repayment of a loan of checkbook money (where only the reserve requirement in lawful money is at risk), if one makes a ten dollar annual interest payment of lawful money on a $100 checkbook money loan then, assuming a 10 percent reserve requirement, the annual interest will be 100 percent, and therefore usurious.

Interest rates are often confusing and deceiving. The annual percentage rate (APR) is the yardstick used to compare costs of loans. Although it does a fairly good job of putting rates in perspective, lenders can still manage to complicate it and make rates deceiving.

In 1968, Congress passed the Truth in Lending Act, which was revised and updated in 1982. This law demands that lenders provide loan applicants with complete and accurate information on the real cost of borrowing money. The borrower must be shown how much he is paying in terms of both percentage and dollar amounts.

In accordance with the Truth in Lending Act, creditors must supply the borrower eighteen distinct disclosures before the loan settlement date, and the first four listed here must be displayed on the papers the borrower signs:

1. The finance charge (including fees and points)
2. The annual percentage rate
3. The amount financed
4. The total amount of all payments
5. Identification of lender
6. Actual payment schedule
7. Late payment charge
8. Prepayment penalty charges, if any
9. Insurance
10. Filing fee
11. Regular collateral
12. Regular deposits
13. Assumability of loan
14. Pay on demand clause
15. Any voidable rate features of loan
16. Total sales price, if seller is also the creditor
17. Itemization of amount financed
18. Reference to any terms shown on the loan contract not shown on the disclosure statement

If the lender does not provide all the foregoing information at the closing of the loan, he has broken the law and can be challenged on any claim he has against you.

Is there a law on the books that gives privately owned commercial banks authority to create lawful money? Is there any law that authorizes banks to create checkbook money and pass it off as lawful money? I have asked these questions of many attorneys who actively practice banking law, and each has assured me that banks cannot create lawful money or, for that matter, any other kind of money. They all assure me that the only authority to create money rests with the United States government. There are court decisions that back up this contention. One must also seriously ask, "What lawful consideration does a bank give a borrower when it creates and lends checkbook money?"

Some attorneys with whom I have consulted are of the opinion, that if banks are actually creating private bank money and "passing it off" as lawful money, then not only is the transaction fraudulent but the debt becomes unlawful. If the debt is unlawful, and the bank sends at least two notices through the mail within a 10-year period to collect an unlawful debt, has not mail fraud and racketeering resulted?

What would happen if everyone who has a loan sues the bank for creating checkbook money and passing it off as lawful money? Will the republic be destroyed? Absolutely not. What millions of such lawsuits will likely do is bring the attention of Congress to our monetary problem. Congress can then intelligently reform the banking system and thus prevent the future failure of the industry. Thus all citizens would benefit from monetary reform.

The world needs monetary reform now, particularly with recent events in Eastern Europe and the festering economic woes in South and Central America. Excessive debt and reckless abuse of and by our banking system must be contained. Archaic and surreptitious banking practices must, out of a sense of morality if nothing else, cease.

Chapter 15

Peace and Plenty

Knowledge in itself is not power. Only when knowledge is cohesively and systematically fueled by emotion, and propelled into action, does it become a powerful force.

Embracing the solution to our flawed monetary system will require acceptance of probably the most vexing concept contained in this book. Monetary stability can be achieved in this country if the national Treasury of the United States creates all money and, more importantly, if the Treasury clears all checks.

Trust the politicians to create money? This conclusion probably brings waves of uneasiness sweeping through those who distrust our elected officials. But, remember we the people are the government, and we ultimately can demand accountability of our elected officials. This notion is idealistic, perhaps, but nevertheless clearly plausible in the case of our money system. To cure our ailing money system, we must be prepared to take dramatic steps.

Our government is stable by virtue of the fact that it is based upon law as opposed to policy. Policies can be changed at the slightest whim. We need stability in our monetary system, so we ought to rely on laws rather than policy to govern the system. Laws with checks and balances must be enacted to prevent governmental abuse of the money creation process. In my opinion, the concept of the government creating money is not vexing at all. The majority of the population already believes that the government is creating our money. I strongly expect that when they are informed that our money problems are caused by the private money creators, the people will demand that the money creation process be placed in the hands of our government.

Balancing the creation of money with its extinguishment ought to be the job of government. Currently, private policy decisions control the money supply. Decisions by the private banking establishment drastically reduce or increase the amount of credit available and cause bust or boom cycles in the economy. A sharp reduction in credit produces a serious economic depression. Policy decisions can encourage or discourage lending by private banks to a particular segment of the economy, causing either prosperity or suffering in that one segment.

Policy is arbitrary. Only when our monetary system is based upon impartial mathematical laws will the system be fair to everyone. The debt monetary system is inherently unstable. On the other hand, our political system is based on the United States Constitution, the most successful document ever devised for a democracy and a model of stability. The Constitution has provisions for the government to create currency and coin, so it only makes sense to examine the concept and explore its possibilities in light of the other overwhelming governmental successes we enjoy as a result of our Constitution.

The Federal Reserve System was born out of a conviction that something needed to be done to bring order into the chaotic banking system that was plaguing the nation at the turn of the century. During the ensuing years, the system was institutionalized, and those opposed to change argued that the Federal Reserve System served America well.

In 1988 the Federal Reserve had an income of $19.5 billion, and it turned back $17.36 billion to the U.S. Treasury as provided under its charter. The Federal Reserve Act of 1913 provided that a substantial portion of the Feds annual profits be turned over to the national Treasury. Does this fact dilute the argument that there are vast profits built into the commercial banking system? No. Consider for a moment that the total debt (public debt plus private debt) at the end of 1988 was in excess of $11 trillion. Then, the discount rate, the rate at which banks can borrow from the Federal Reserve, was about 9.4 percent. Assuming the debt carried the same rate as the discount rate, there was an annual interest charge of almost $1 trillion on the total debt owed to the banking system.

While all of this interest payment does not go to commercial banks, an overwhelmingly large part of it does. The $17.36 billion turned over to the U.S. Treasury is thus much less than 2 percent of the total carrying charge on the total debt. If you are mystified by large numbers, look at it this way. Assume you receive $17 from your central bank, but the charge they require you to pay is over $900 in interest on a debt of $10,000, which they created out of thin air. Now can you appreciate what is happening?

If there exists a basic distrust of government in America, that distrust is fueled by the caustic rhetoric in the media as well as partisan political debate in the Congress. Media criticism is aimed at the government's inability to solve monetary problems, which are currently insoluble because of the flaw in our monetary system. When Congress is condemned for its monetary policy, the criticism is part of a "condemn and divide" axis that wrongly condemns politicians for too much spending when their major sin is too much borrowing. Besides, Congress is not responsible for monetary policy; but it is unfairly blamed for the actions of the privately owned Federal Reserve System.

The solution is a system that would provide adequate funds for government without borrowing; a system that would likewise effectively eliminate income taxes and build trust in our elected officials. Critics of this approach will sound their distrust of the "politicians." But the reforms suggested will measurably increase the faith our citizens have in our elected officials because they will remove many of the causes of criticism. For example, our public officials should be paid on a level equal to the wages paid by industry for comparable jobs. Is this the case today? Prior to a recent wage hike, congresspersons made $70,000 per year; yet they are expected to maintain two residences—one in Washington, D.C., and another in their respective district. They are expected to follow a lifestyle that requires a level of income much higher than that provided. They should be paid a fair salary—one that would preclude accepting fees for speeches or "moonlighting" to bring in extra funds.

Congressional salaries is clearly an area that can lead to significant abuse, and the debate over it causes severe criticism from citizens. Why? Currently, the funds to pay the salaries of elected officials come from the government's taxing authority. But without taxes, and with government creating debt-free money for all of its expenditures, elected officials could be paid a fair wage without picking the pockets of the citizens. Would there then be any objection to adequate salaries?

Our elected officials are severely criticized for spending. I repeat, though, spending for worthwhile public projects is no transgression. The sin is too much borrowing for public projects.

Prosperity is a sure cure for many of the problems we face today, and it is reasonable to conclude that we will enjoy greater prosperity in America when we call a halt to the interest payments and taxes that must be paid when our government borrows. The ever-increasing debt is the core reason we distrust our political officials. But they have been wrestling with problems that are unsolvable within an all-debt monetary system. What we understand as incompetence is nothing more than the frustration society experiences when confronted with a difficult problem—a problem that defies solution under current monetary practice.

At this point, you might legitimately ask, "What should we use for money?" If the Federal Reserve System has demonstrated one major point, it has shown that coins, currency, and checkbook money can work extremely well as a medium of exchange. The compelling need is only to remove the authority for creating this medium of exchange from the privately owned banks and to place it in the hands of the national Treasury where it belongs according to the Constitution.

It is time to recognize that our hardworking public officials have been working on our monetary problems for some time but that their efforts have been misdirected. Their advisors do not know any more about the problem than they do. They have unknowingly confronted a problem that in the present framework is insoluble. And Congress collectively reflects the general public's lack of information about our monetary system. The absence of trust in our public officials has been caused by the public's perception of their impeded progress in solving the problem.

The Truth about Inflation

Nonproductive interest payments to the money creators that reduce the circulating M1 is the primary cause of inflation.

The popular belief is that inflation is caused by too much money chasing too few goods in the economy. People who hold this view have not identified the debt-dominant character of our monetary system. As a result of this fallacious thinking, the policies of the Federal Reserve System during a sustained inflationary period are directed toward reducing the money supply in the economy. In reality, an element of debt-free money should be spent directly into circulation in amounts to compensate for the continual removal of money from the M1 to pay nonproductive usury, or interest. This infusion will not wipe out inflation, but it will prevent economic recessions, depressions, bankruptcies, foreclosures, and unemployment.

There is a pervasive body of opinion that holds that the prosperity that occurs during an inflationary period must be counteracted by a recession; a period of well-being must be dampened by a period of reduced economic activity that results in business failures and unemployment. This basic misconception is held up as a truth in our present economic thinking. Common sense would lead thoughtful people to disagree with such a concept.

When you enter the parking lot of a car dealership, you are besieged by car salesmen trying to sell you a car. Many of the salesmen will "wheel and deal" on price and features. The car dealerships hold sales continuously, and many are willing to give "rebates" of $1,000 to $2,500 so that you will part with your money and haul their auto away. Just who is chasing what here? Is the money chasing the product, or the product chasing the money? There is no shortage of cars, yet prices for cars that keep getting smaller and smaller keep going up and up. Inflation is occurring despite the fact that there is more than an adequate supply of products.

The same holds true for the myriad of products advertised on television, radio, and in the newspapers. Prices for products keep going up from year to year even though there is no shortage of these products. Inflation is not caused by too much money chasing too few products. This statement simply does not square with what goes on in the marketplace. If this were true, how would economists explain the phenomenon of an "inflationary recession" when they all believe that a recession is caused by a shortage of money? An inflationary recession implies that there is simultaneously too much money and too little money in the economy. This is not possible. In the United States, products are always chasing money, except in isolated auctions.

For the sake of argument, suppose there is too much money in the hands of manufacturers, retailers, and consumers. How would this fact create price inflation of goods and services? Have you ever seen consumers standing around an auctioneer, in a supermarket or department store, or car dealership bidding up prices? Of course not. There has to be another explanation for inflation.

In a microcosmic economic community where consumers have large sums of money in their possession and there is a limited supply of products, prices for products could be bid upwards and produce price inflation. This situation sometimes occurs at small, private auctions. Such a phenomenon, however, does not occur in an open market economy where goods and services are plentiful—the system found in the United States. Even given an expanded money supply in the hands of the consumers, manufacturers and retailers will still price their goods according to the costs of those goods, plus a reasonable profit margin. Prices are not based on the amount of money floating around in the economy. Besides, how would the manufacturers and retailers even know when there was an overabundance of money?

Another microcosmic example of inflation can be seen in "price gouging," which sometimes occurs during natural disasters such as hurricanes and earthquakes when large and unusual demands for certain goods and services are created. Of course, a currency devaluation instantaneously causes inflation. This occurred in Venezuela and Argentina in March and May 1989, respectively.

Auctions and price gouging, which produce temporary and very limited inflation on specific items is not a true cause of a general price inflation of goods and services. A currency devaluation, does, however, produce generalized price inflation immediately. Profits, increased wages, and greed are secondary causes of inflation. As long as humans suffer from greed, desiring more than they can provide for themselves, inflation will always remain in society. Inflation is the result of human beings disregarding Newton's Law: "For every action, there is an equal and opposite reaction."

One might legitimately ask why the M1 increases during an inflationary trend. Does this increase in the M1 during an inflationary phase in our economy cause prices to go up? On the contrary, the increase in the M1 during inflation is because increased borrowing is necessary to pay the usurious debt service and to facilitate the exchange of goods and services from manufacturer to retailer to consumer. If this borrowing does not occur to increase the M1, then consumers will be short of money because of the decreasing size of the M1 caused by interest payments to the banks. Consumers will not be able to move products from the shelves of supermarkets or department stores and inventories will pile up. The manufacturers will have to decrease production and lay off their work force. It is thus falsely perceived that an increase in the M1 is the cause of price increases during the expansionary phase of the economy.

Do employee wage increases cause inflation. The answer is, "no." Wage increases usually occur because of inflation and not because of increased production. Inflation and wage increases produce a vicious cycle—one fueling the other. Inflation occurs first, and wage increases follow to keep pace with a rising consumer price index. The consumer price index is a measure of inflation or a measure of how fast money is losing its purchasing power.

In the mid-1970s, oil prices escalated rapidly. The Middle East removed a large part of the purchasing power from this country when United States dollars flowed into the coffers of the Middle Eastern nations. The circulating M1 was greatly decreased. In 1980 we suffered extraordinary rates of inflation. Prices rose to meet the costs of debt service—interest! This inflation occurred in spite of the removal of money from the United States economy; the missing part of the monetary equation, the mountainous debt that increases daily, is the component that eludes traditional economic scholars about the true cause of inflation.

In our monetary system, a portion of the M1 must be spent debt-free into the economy. Without an adequate supply of debt-free money in the economy, recession and depression can never be halted. The only way these continuing horrors can be wiped out is for a controlled portion of the money supply to be spent debt-free into the economy on a regular basis.

Inflation, on the other hand, can be favorably controlled but not totally wiped out. It can, however, be controlled without creating economic recessions and depressions and their deadly side effects, such as bankruptcies, foreclosures, and unemployment. If aggregate interest payments can be reduced, then inflation will be controlled. Reduction of interest payments can be achieved as follows:

Since the national Treasury will be creating debt-free money for its expenditures, government will not be competing with the private sector for funds; therefore, interest rates will drop. In addition, since there will be no shortage of funds in the economic arena to pay interest, the private sector will have no need to borrow to make interest payments and to facilitate the exchange of goods and services. Because income taxes will be eliminated, manufacturers, retailers, and consumers will have more tax-free dollars in their pockets. This will further decrease borrowings from banks, and the decrease in borrowing will lead to a decrease in aggregate interest payments to banks. The cost of doing business will also decrease, further curtailing inflation.

Can a totally stable purchasing power of money be achieved? Yes, but only after inflation is totally wiped out, and the demise of inflation cannot be legislated. Its demise will occur naturally when human beings evolve through mutual respect and love for one another, regardless of color, class, or creed, so that we care for others like we care for ourselves—if not more—in other words, when we live a life of love and giving instead of hate and greed.

A balanced monetary system where the M1 is made up of a combination of debt-free and debt-money is the only way recessions and severe swings in the economy can be diminished and eventually wiped out. Reducing expenditures, increasing taxes, borrowing, or devaluing currencies are not the answers to the inherent problems of our debt-dominant monetary system. These are only quick, temporary fixes.

I have demonstrated that in an all-debt money system there comes a time when the annual compound interest on a borrowed amount of money grows to a sum greater than the original principal. Although money is not an element of nature and does not grow on trees, it certainly grows as debt. When the time comes when the amount of annual interest due on the public debt is greater than the amount of money in circulation, total financial collapse is imminent. Reducing expenditures and increasing taxes are only first-aid measures when, instead, the patient needs a complete transplant!

A World Without Income Tax

In a balanced monetary system administered by the national Treasury for the benefit of all the people, there is no need for an income tax, death and estate taxes, or most other taxes—and certainly no need for the Internal Revenue Service. President Ronald Reagan was elected because he promised lower taxes. He promised tax reform, which was enacted in 1986, but I wonder how many Americans realized that our taxes went up instead of down with that reform act.

President Bush was elected on the slogan, "Read my lips—no new taxes." But in June of 1990, Bush too agreed to increase taxes, even though both he and Reagan had already raided the Social Security trust funds to make their budget deficit spending look less on paper. In addition, President Bush's chief economic advisor and his budget director apparently know little about the science of money. I would not expect Bush to know much about money, but I do hold his advisors accountable. They advised Bush that there are only three ways for the government to get money: increase taxes, cut current expenditures, or borrow. They've probably not heard of debt-free money created by the national Treasury nor have they investigated the monetary policies of the Channel Islands. They also have not asked monetary scientists to advise the president.

"Tax Freedom Day" occurs sometime in June for most of us. On that day, you quit working for your government and get to work for yourself, taking home all your paycheck. The first five and one-half months of the year you spend working for the government. After "Tax Freedom Day," however, you are still not free to keep all you earn. You still have to pay sales tax, property tax, and a host of other taxes. In feudal times, one only gave up 25 percent of what one earned. It's hard to imagine keeping all your earnings on a regular basis for the whole year but it is possible if you want it.

Prior to 1916, the United States had no income tax. Our income tax rate started at 0.5 percent and was intended to be in force for a short time only. Instead, taxation seems to have become a permanent fixture, and the rate is increasing. In 1929, Tax Freedom Day was February 9. In 1940, it was March 8. In 1960, it was April 17. And now that our president has agreed to increase taxes again, it's anyone's guess when Tax Freedom Day will be in 1991. Now that the trend to increase taxes has been set, one has to be terribly naive to think that the trend will not continue. When will Tax Freedom Day be in years 1995, 2000, and 2012?

Consider the wrenching problems that have resulted from the United States income tax. Without this tax, there would be no need for financial people to consider "junk bonds" as a way to avoid taxes. (Interest on bonds is a deductible business expense and allows a business to deduct interest payments against revenues, whereas revenues earned are taxed and then passed on to shareholders in the form of dividends—and then taxed again.)

Twelve percent of senior citizens live below poverty level, and these are people who for the most part have led sane, productive lives. Why are they in this condition? A part of their earnings was removed in the form of taxes, and the Social Security "insurance" their government provided was ravaged by inflation. Inflation is a cruel specter faced by older Americans on fixed incomes. Furthermore, because of the continually rising appetite for taxes in America due to the burgeoning debt, social security benefits are being taxed for some Americans who have successfully funded their retirement.

Increased taxes are needed to pay the interest on government debt. If government had no debt and consequently no interest payments, there would be no need for such taxes. If there were no tax code and the Congress did not have to wrestle constantly with increasing levels of debt, wouldn't the government function more smoothly and thus enjoy more credibility?

When the Internal Revenue Service is eliminated and all taxes are removed, 100 percent of corporate profits will be available for use by corporations. The increase in overall prosperity will be astounding as corporate profits increase by the amount of the former tax on profits.

If abolishing taxes sounds outlandish, remember that income taxes were not instituted until 1916. America functioned quite well for over 140 years without a tax on income. If the removal of income taxes negated the need for the Internal Revenue Service, who would object?

The problem in the United States today is not too much spending, it is too much borrowing. Eliminate government borrowing at interest and elected officials can begin to address the concerns of society rather than serve as referees between the various special-interest groups. This constant conflict is devisive and impedes the progress of government. Remove the cause of the governmental conflicts, and citizens' confidence in their officials' ability to govern effectively and honestly will rise dramatically. Gone, too, would be the constant harping about who is "paying their fair share" of taxes. I believe that the numbers who maintain a basic distrust of government will dwindle to a disgruntled minority, probably beneficiaries of the current, all-debt monetary system. Make no mistake, the debt-dominant money system is a festering wound that will eventually cause monumental destruction to society. Our elected officials have a wonderful opportunity today to seize the initiative and demand that our rights be restored so that we can confront our real problems rather than confronting those we elect to serve us.

The Federal Reserve System was created in 1913, and the act that created the income tax in America was not passed until 1916. The insatiable demand for funds to meet debt obligations has resulted in some staggering increases in the income taxes since it was first imposed in 1916. At one time the "marginal tax rate" in this country was 90 percent. A marginal tax was the tax levied on any additonal dollars above a set annual income. Between the years 1944 and 1945 the 90 percent marginal rate applied to all income above $200,000 per year.

Our government tries to create a balanced budget while continuing to provide various services. In a balanced monetary system administered by the national Treasury, there will be no lack of funds for any needed, achievable, and authorized public projects. The government will have almost unlimited monetary resources for its defense projects, for social programs, for health and education programs, for space and other research and development programs, for fighting foreign wars, and the domestic war against drugs. This "newfound" money will come from the government's greatest creative opportunity as provided in Article 1, Section 8, Clause 5 of the U.S. Constitution—the right to coin (create) and regulate the value of money.

The government will be able to resume its space program full steam ahead without worrying where funds come from. If the government needs additional funding for its projects, it will create debt-free money and spend it into circulation. Will this excess money cause inflation? No, it is exactly this debt-free expenditure that is needed to control inflation and to help prevent economic recessions and depressions and their unwanted consequences.

With almost unlimited, authorized debt-free funds available for expenditure, the United States can have the strongest defense system in the world. Why should there be a shortage of money when it doesn't take any raw materials to create it? Our current money system has no precious metal backing. All we need is paper, ink, numbers, and a computer.

Cultivating the Greatest Resource

The greatest natural resource on our planet is human beings—human beings with inquisitive minds and healthy bodies. Today, millions of Americans are unable to afford health care because they are unemployed and have no health insurance. In fact, forty million Americans are currently without health insurance.

This problem is encountered in doctors' offices and hospital emergency rooms across the United States. Medicare and Medicaid programs are in jeopardy because the government is cutting back on benefits in these two programs. Private health care programs are also in jeopardy, becoming more expensive and with benefits to subscribers decreasing annually. These cutbacks are not a result of the government and the private sector having too much money. No worthwhile program is slashed because there is too much money. The cuts are a result of lack of funds.

In June 1990, President Bush agreed to substantially decrease Medicare and Medicaid funding to reduce deficit spending in the national budget. The state of Oregon has already passed a law to ration health care for the elderly. The federal government is considering similar laws for the nation as a whole. Who will then determine who lives and who dies? We are quickly moving to a socialized health care system in which our standard of health care is bound to go down in a country in which the highest possible standards for everything is not only expected but is demanded. Our national medical and dental associations, who are also ignorant about how money works, are quietly accepting governmental decisions about reduced health care. These organizations and their members complain but have no solutions to these problems.

Not only are we racing toward a mediocre health care system, but we're heading toward a mediocre standard of living in general. No business fails because it has too much money. Individuals do not declare bankruptcy because they have too much money. The problem is universal, and the cause is always the same—a shortage of money, that commodity created out of the thin air and generally without labor.

Why isn't the problem solved? The answer is simple: The science of money is understood by only a handful of people, the very people who are being universally ignored! When the government starts to spend debt-free money into our economy, there will be no shortage of money for the care of the indigent and the elderly.

Higher education should be fostered and nurtured by the government, for the strength of our nation depends upon its citizens. The greatest resource of any nation is its people. But there are too many people struggling to get an education in this country because they are unable to pay for it. This is a national tragedy. In addition, salaries should be increased to attract better teachers for our schools to save our deteriorating educational system.

A system should be set up so that those willing and able to receive a higher education have that opportunity, whether they can pay for it or not. Educated people become assets for the whole country. Understand, I am not advocating communism, but for the benefit of the country as a whole, one should be willing to tap every resource possible, especially the human resource. There is no logical reason the government cannot provide free education for those willing and able to receive it.

Governmental programs can be expanded so that we can direct our creative energies toward exploring the depths of the oceans, the vast outer reaches of the universe, and the final frontier—our minds. By eliminating money shortages, we can provide for the health and education of all human beings in this country. We can each design a plan for our lives, instead of eking out a living on a planet of abundance, in a system where many of us are destined to fail no matter how hard and honestly we work.

With plenty of money to activate the production of goods and services and with the mobilization of population groups from infertile lands to fertile lands, poverty, disease, and starvation can be eliminated. Humankind can set civilization on a steadfast course toward a peaceful future of plenty where we belong, for remember, our flawed monetary system is responsible for the shortage of money, the root of most of the evils present on this planet.

Liberty and Free Enterprise

With the money creation process in the hands of all the people, there will exist a true free enterprise system in the marketplace, and when people fail, their failure will be a result of their own doing and not because of a lack of debt-free money in the economy. Everyone will be encouraged to compete freely, and everyone will earn according to his ability and willingness to work. No one will gain at the expense of another because of the way the system is constructed. The limits on what or how much one will earn will be set by the individual and not by anyone else or by the system.

I advocate an honest, unrestrained free enterprise system under a balanced monetary system, administered by all the people through their own Congress. In the current all-debt or debt-dominant monetary system, the power of compound interest will eventually transfer all the wealth of the country into the hands of the money creators through bankruptcies and foreclosures. It is only a matter of time. When this occurs, will there be a reason to maintain a democracy? Will there be any reason to have more than one political party? Will there be any reason to have a national election? Is not the likely result of the all-debt monetary system a totalitarian form of government? Who will be the rulers—the government, or the money creators? Or will they be one and the same? After all, history has shown that those who control the tangible wealth rule!

Perhaps it is time to throw away the useless rhetorical dichotomies of booms and busts, haves and have nots, up-swings and downturns, Republicans and Democrats. We must investigate and embrace the truth of a balanced monetary system. Once such a system is adopted, our government will at once be truly a government "of the people, by the people, for the people," as so eloquently expressed by Lincoln.

America has been characterized as "the land of the free and the home of the brave." It is time we claim that promise.

Freedom anyone?

End Notes

Chapter 1

1. Batra, Ravi, *The Great Depression of 1990* (New York: Simon and Schuster, 1987).
2. Friedman, D. H., and C. J. Parnow, *The Story of Money* (New York: Federal Reserve Bank of New York, 1984).
3. Batra, *Depression.*

Chapter 2

1. Federal Reserve Bank of New York, *Money: Master or Servant* (New York: Federal Reserve Bank of New York, 1984).
2. Federal Reserve Bank of New York, *I Bet You Thought*, 4th ed. (New York: Federal Reserve Bank of New York, 1984).
3. Friedman, D. H., and C. J. Parnow, *The Story of Money* (New York: Federal Reserve Bank of New York, 1984).
4. Fed. Res. of N. Y., *I Bet.*
5. Fed Res. of N. Y., *I Bet.*
6. *Federal Reserve Act*, Board of Governors of the Federal Reserve, Section 7, Clause 3.

7. *Lewis vs. United States*, 680 F 2nd 1239, 1982, US Reports.

8. U. S. Congress, House Committee on Banking and Currency, *The Federal Reserve System after 50 Years: Proposals for the Improvement of the Federal Reserve* (Washington, D.C.: House Committee on Banking and Currency, 1964).

9. House Committe on Banking and Currency, *Proposals for Improvement.*

10. *Treasury Monetarist* (Wickliffe, Ohio: Monetary Science Publishers, 1985).

11. Subcommittee on Domestic Finance of the House Committee on Banking and Currency, *A Primer on Money* (Washington, D.C.: Subcommittee on Domestic Finance of the Committee on Banking and Currency, 1964).

12. Fed. Res. of N.Y., *Money: Master or Servant.*

13. House Subcommittee on Finance, *Primer.*

14. Samuelson, Paul A., *Ecomomics, An Introductory Analysis*, 9th ed. (New York: McGraw-Hill, 1973).

15. Federal Reserve Bank of Chicago, *Modern Money Mechanics* (Chicago: Federal Reserve of Chicago, 1982).

Chapter 3

1. House Committee on Banking and Currency, *Money Facts* (Washington, D.C.: Committee on Banking and Currency, 1964).

2. House Committee on Banking and Currency, *Money Facts.*

3. Federal Reserve Bank of Chicago, *Modern Money Mechanics* (Chicago: Federal Reserve Bank of Chicago, 1982).

4. Federal Reserve Bank of New York, *Money: Master or Servant* (New York: Federal Reserve Bank of New York, 1984).

5. Federal Reserve Bank of N.Y., *Money: Master or Servant*.

6. Federal Reserve Bank of San Francisco, *Monetary Policy in the United States* (San Francisco: Federal Reserve Bank of San Francisco, 1987).

7. Federal Reserve Bank of San Francisco, *Policy*.

Chapter 4

1. Bankinvest, *Precis* (Zurich: Bankinvest, 1976).

2. Omni Publications, *Lincoln—Money Martyred* (Hawthorne: Omni Publications, 1935).

Chapter 7

1. Omni Publications, *Lightning over the Treasury Building* (Hawthorne: Omni Publications).

2. Dwinell, Olive C, *The Story of Our Money* (Boston: Forum Publishing Company, 1946).

3. U. S. Congress, Senate, *National Economic and Banking System of the United States*, 76th Congress, 1st session, Senate Document 23.

4. *Annals of Congress*, (vol. 1, 1790).

5. *Great Thoughts* (New York: Ballantine Books, 1985).

6. *Economic Report of the President* (Washington, D.C.: United States government Printing Office, 1987).

7. Omni Publications, *The Legalized Crime of Banking and a Constitutional Remedy* (Hawthorne: Omni Publications, 1976).

Chapter 8

1. Subcommittee on Domestic Finance of the House Committee on Banking and Currency, *A Primer on Money* (Washington, D.C.: Subcommittee on Domestic Finance of the Committee on Banking and Currency, 1964).
2. Federal Reserve Bank of New York, *The Story of Banks and Thrifts* (New York: Federal Reserve Bank of New York, Public Information Department, 1985).

Chapter 9

1. Neeley, Karen, *Texas Bank Director's Handbook* (Temple: Texas Bankers Association, 1984).
2. Royal Commission, *The Mirror* (Auckland: The Mirror Publishing Company, 1955).
3. Towers, Graham, *Hearings on Domestic Finance and Banking* (Ottawa: Canadian Government Printing Office, 1939).
4. Subcommittee on Domestic Finance of the House Committee on Banking and Currency, *Primer on Money* (Washington, D.C.: Subcommittee on Domestic Finance of the Committee on Banking and Currency, 1964).
5. Monetary Science Publishing, *The Treasury Monetarist* (Wickliffe: Monetary Science Publishing, 1989).
6. Monetary Science, *Monetarist*.
7. Monetary Science, *Monetarist*.
8. *Putting It Simply* (Boston: Federal Reserve Bank of Boston, 1986).
9. *I Bet You Thought*, 4th ed. (New York: Federal Reserve Bank of New York, 1984).

Chapter 11

1. *Report to the Congress of the Commission on the Role of Gold in the Domestic and International Monetary System* (Washington, D.C.: Government Printing Office, 1982), Vol. II, p. 342.

2. *United States Treasury Bulletin* (Washington, D.C.: Government Printing Office, 1976).

3. *Federal Reserve Bulletin* (Washington, D.C.: Government Printing Office, 1987).

4. Federal Reserve Bank of New York, *I Bet You Thought* (New York: Federal Reserve Bank of New York, 1984)

Chapter 12

1. Lightning over the Treasury Building.

2. Nordskog, Andrae, *We Bankers.*

3. Holzapfel, Karl, *The New Federalist Newspaper* (Washington, D.C., May 1989).

4. Ibid.

5. Buffett, Warren, "How Inflation Robs the Equity Investor," *Fortune* magazine, May 1971.

Chapter 14

1. F and PR vs. Richmond, 133 SE 888; 144 SE 501, 151 Va. 195.

2. Community Federal Saving and Loan vs. Fields, 128 F 2nd 705 (*Black's Law Dictionary*, 5th edition).

3. Merchants' Bank vs. Baird, 160 F 642.

4. First National Bank of Tallapoosa vs. Monroe, 135 GA 614, 69 SE 1123, 32LRA (NS) f 550.

5. Morton Grocery Co. vs. People's National Bank, 144 SE 501, 151 Va 195.

6. Morse, *Banks and Banking*, 5th edition, Section 65; Magee, *Banks and Banking*, 3rd edition, Section 248; American Express Company vs. Citizens State Bank, 194 NW 429.

INDEX

239